"Cameron Cole candidly offers practical and biblical advice for those who mourn in *Therefore I Have Hope*. An easy-to-read work without heavy theological language, this book can be understood and immediately applied to make a difference in a mourner's life. Cole openly shares lessons he's learning following the tragic loss of his son and does not shy away from gradually and carefully pulling back the curtain on very real and present pain. The principles he shares apply to those who suffer various losses—the loss of a job, a parent, a child, one's identity, one's confidence, or one's friends."

Robert Smith Jr., Charles T. Carter Baptist Chair of Divinity, Beeson Divinity School, Samford University

"With both sensitivity and skill, Cameron Cole proves in this book that the central truths of the Bible actually matter for those of us who have ever encountered the often unspeakable tragedies of life. While our words to ourselves and to those who encounter suffering and loss sometimes fall flat, Cole reminds us that the profound realities found in the person and work of Jesus Christ and his resurrection can lift us to new heights of faith, hope, and love. Every Christian needs to read this book to discover anew that God is both great and good—no matter what may befall us."

Julius J. Kim, Dean of Students, Professor of Practical Theology, Westminster Seminary California

"Suffering and grief accumulate. No wonder we live in a time when many have lost the landmarks of faith, hope, and love due to overwhelming heartache. Cameron Cole's book *Therefore I Have Hope* does not shirk from confronting tragedy. His own story of loss is almost unbearable. *Almost*. But this book does not leave us drowning in the inevitable question of, "Where is God?" or suffocating in trivial answers. Cole deftly intersects God's own stories with ours to light the lamps of faith, hope, and love."

Sharon Hersh, Adjunct Professor of Counseling, Reformed Theological Seminary, Orlando; author, *Begin Again, Believe Again*

"Having lost my father when I was eighteen and my brother several years later to suicide, I've walked the lonely road of grief. I only wish I'd had a resource like Cameron Cole's book, which is hopeful without being trite and biblical without being preachy. This book will be of such immense encouragement and help, not just because it's hopeful but because it's *human*. I marvel that Cole bears such compelling witness to God's grace in the midst of his Worst, and I can't wait to put this book into the hands of people who, like Job, wonder if God has disappeared."

Jen Pollock Michel, author, *Teach Us to Want* and *Keeping Place*

"*Therefore I Have Hope* chronicles Cameron Cole's journey into one of the hardest stories a parent will ever experience, the death of a child. But, thankfully, it's a journey that didn't get sabotaged by graceless cynicism or religious cliché. The gospel of God's grace is more beautiful and believable to me having read Cameron's book. I cannot wait to share this story, these painful tears, and this profound joy."

Scotty Ward Smith, Pastor Emeritus, Christ Community Church, Franklin, Tennessee; Teacher in Residence, West End Community Church, Nashville, Tennessee

"The problem of suffering is a plaything for philosophers but a reality for humans. Here, in the raw pain of grief, Cameron Cole shows God's way of enabling Christians to face the reality of suffering. Cameron shows how the great truths of God's Word prepare, enable, and equip us to live by hope in the midst of tragedy. A good book to read before our Worst confronts us."

Phillip Jensen, Former Dean of Sydney, St. Andrew's Cathedral

"In a world on the precipice of despair, we need a clear theology of suffering so we might truly live out a transformational theology of hope. Stories like Cole's embody the type of flourishing available on the other side of our very worst fears, and this book offers practical ways to find a hope that does not put us to shame no matter what storms may come."

Jay and Katherine Wolf, Founders, HOPE HEALS; authors, *Hope Heals: A True Story of Overwhelming Loss and an Overcoming Love*

Therefore I Have Hope

Therefore I Have Hope

12 Truths That Comfort, Sustain, and Redeem in Tragedy

Cameron Cole

WHEATON, ILLINOIS

Therefore I Have Hope: 12 Truths That Comfort, Sustain, and Redeem in Tragedy

Published by Crossway
1300 Crescent Street
Wheaton, Illinois 60187

Cover design: Crystal Courtney

Cover image: Zak Shelhamer

First printing 2018

Printed in the United States of America

All emphases in Scripture quotations have been added by the author.

Trade paperback ISBN: 978-1-4335-5877-1
ePub ISBN: 978-1-4335-5880-1
PDF ISBN: 978-1-4335-5878-8
Mobipocket ISBN: 978-1-4335-5879-5

Library of Congress Cataloging-in-Publication Data

Names: Cole, Cameron, 1979- author.
Title: Therefore I have hope : 12 truths that comfort, sustain, and redeem in tragedy / Cameron Cole.
Description: Wheaton : Crossway, 2018. | Includes bibliographical references and index.
Identifiers: LCCN 2017060547 (print) | LCCN 2018021204 (ebook) | ISBN 9781433558788 (pdf) | ISBN 9781433558795 (mobi) | ISBN 9781433558801 (epub) | ISBN 9781433558771 (tp)
Subjects: LCSH: Children—Death—Religious aspects—Christianity. | Loss (Psychology)—Religious aspects—Christianity. | Grief—Religious aspects—Christianity. | Bereavement—Religious aspects—Christianity. | Consolation.
Classification: LCC BV4907 (ebook) | LCC BV4907 .C645 2018 (print) | DDC 248.8/6—dc23
LC record available at https://lccn.loc.gov/2017060547

Crossway is a publishing ministry of Good News Publishers.

VP 28 27 26 25 24 23 22 21 20 19 18
14 13 12 11 10 9 8 7 6 5 4 3 2

To my precious little boy, Cameron,
I will see you again.
And to my wife, Lauren, an amazing friend,
and, in the end, a courageous one too.

Contents

Foreword

I wonder how I would respond if the worst thing I could imagine happened to me?

Those were my thoughts, many years ago, that I expressed aloud to a small group as we studied the book of Job. As we read together that Job's initial response to the loss of everything he owned and nearly everyone he loved was that he "arose and tore his robe and shaved his head and fell on the ground and worshiped" in Job 1:20, I wondered, *How did he do that?* As I read the words he uttered in his worship, "Naked I came from my mother's womb, and naked shall I return. The LORD gave, and the LORD has taken away; blessed be the name of the LORD" (v. 21), I wondered, *How could he be so open-handed with what God had given to him?* I couldn't help but wonder what my initial response to incredible loss might be if and when it came my way. I didn't think it would be worship. But I wanted it to be.

Two weeks later I gave birth to a daughter we named Hope. On the second day of her life, we found out that her life would be very short and very difficult. I remember waking up the following morning and thinking to myself, *I guess this is my chance. This is where I'm going to find out how I will respond when the worst thing I can imagine happens to me.*

Perhaps you've been there too, or find yourself there right now, wondering how you are going to respond to, as Cameron puts it in the pages that follow, "your Worst." Or perhaps your life has been relatively sorrow-free, and you find yourself living with a nagging fear of the day when your Worst happens to you. Perhaps you find yourself wondering what impact the inevitable losses and sorrows of this life will have on your happy life, your sense of self, your relationships, and your ability to trust in God.

As I studied the book of Job during my daughter's brief life, I discovered that a key to Job's faithful response was the tight grip he had on what he knew to be true about God. He also admitted that his understanding of who God is and what God is doing in the world—especially in terms of suffering—was incredibly limited. It was his security in what he knew about God and his submission to what he didn't understand about God that enabled Job to be confident that, "when he has tried me, I shall come out as gold" (Job 23:10).

What is stunning to me, however, is how little revelation Job had to go on. He didn't have the writings of Moses, or the psalms of David, or the promises of the Prophets. He didn't have the record of God himself entering into the suffering of this world that we have in the Gospels, or the application of gospel truths in the epistles, or the confident hope of suffering one day coming to an end that is provided in Revelation.

But we do!

We have so much more than Job had to help us endure difficult days and emerge from this broken world and our Worst with solid hope and confidence in God.

It is this divine Word, this rich revelation, that Cameron Cole has mined, not only to make sense of his own loss and sorrow, but to help all of us make sense of our own. Sometimes when we find ourselves in the confusion of difficulty and the heartbreak of loss, we know that we're supposed to find strength in reading the Bible, but we can't figure out where to start to find it. We know there are truths in it that are meant to instill hope in the midst of heartbreak, but we hurt too much to search for it. We need someone to serve up truth we can chew on. We need someone to point the way toward genuine hope. That's what Cameron does in the pages of this book.

My prayer for you as you begin is that the truths in this book will bring comfort to the deep hurt, sustain you for the long haul, redeem the unimaginable, and fill you with hope in who God is and what he has promised.

Nancy Guthrie
April 2018

Introduction

Like most people, my mind sometimes wanders to places of doom, to places where my imagination entertains (what I perceive to be) *the Worst*. In my adult life, I had made this mental journey enough times that my Worst had developed with vivid detail.

My Worst was likely the same as that of many parents: the persistent fear that my child would die. But my Worst had a second layer for me.

As a youth pastor, I worried that my faith did not possess enough fortitude. God had given me a relatively comfortable life. Any white American male like me, raised in an affluent, stable Christian family, for whom friendships, sports, school, and career had come easily, surely would believe that God is good. I feared that if my Worst occurred, I would lose my faith. I would turn my back on God and walk away from Christianity, and, consequently, my spiritual failure would shatter the faith of hundreds of students to whom I had proclaimed the promises of Christ for over a decade.

My Worst, indeed, entered my life as tragically as I ever imagined it could.

My Worst

On Sunday, November 10, 2013, finding my three-year-old son's lost Lego ax prompted the most magical conversation of my life. After recovering his coveted toy, my three-year-old son, Cam, exclaimed, "Thank you, Jesus! Thank you, Jesus!"

Out of nowhere, my little boy started to ask serious spiritual questions. He asked if we could go see Jesus. When I explained that, while we couldn't see him, Jesus is always with us, he asked if we could drive to see Jesus. After explaining to Cam that we would see Jesus when we got to heaven, my son turned his attention to heaven.

Cam asked if we would see Adam and Eve in heaven. He then declared, "I'm not gonna eat that apple."

My wife and I reminded Cam that we all "eat the apple." We reminded him that God sent Jesus because we all make the same mistake as Adam and Eve did: we all sin.

The conversation ended with my son saying, "Jesus died on cross. Jesus died my sins." In the minutes following that sweet proclamation, my wife, Lauren, and I realized that we had witnessed the dearest dream of every Christian parent—our son had professed faith in Christ.

That night I went on a short, overnight campout with a leader and some students. I awoke on Monday, November 11, to three missed calls from my wife in the span of a minute. I then encountered a voice of terror.

My Worst had entered.

My wife pleaded for me to drive to the children's hospital as soon as possible but offered no explanation. I pressed her for more information until she reluctantly delivered the worst news of my life: "Cam is dead."

Lauren had found our perfectly healthy child lifeless in his bed. Paramedics were attempting to resuscitate him, but she assured me that it was futile. In what remains a medical mystery, our three-year-old child inexplicably died in his sleep, something that occurs to one in a hundred thousand children over the age of one. My child's profession of faith was the last meaningful conversation I ever would have with him on earth. Our son's life had ended in the blink of an eye.

The first half of my dreadful daydreams had become a reality. I had imagined this moment hundreds of times. Here was the point of departure between God and me. Here was that moment when my faith would crumble. In my imagination of doom, here was when I would curse God, resign from ministry, and pursue a life of self-interest as a bitter, faithless man.

But the Lord put a word in my mouth that surprised me. When Lauren delivered the tragic news, I said to her, "Lauren, Christ is risen from the dead. God is good. This doesn't change that fact." God gave me faith and hope while I stood squarely in the middle of my Worst.

The Narrative of Hope

That initial proclamation stood as the first of many moments of hopefulness as I discovered that God had been preparing me for such a tragedy during my entire life. Knowing that this day would come, God used lessons from Bible studies, conversations, theological reading, sermon podcasts, and previous trials to build a foundation that would stand when an overpowering wave of tragedy struck my life.

Throughout the journey of my worst nightmare—my descent into a dark, sad valley—the Holy Spirit would remind me of truths that comforted my soul and sustained my life. Very often in the month after Cam died, I would say to my wife or a friend that I could not conceive how anyone could survive such pain if they did not believe certain biblical principles.

How could a person survive if one did not know the gospel? How could one subsist if one did not accept the sovereignty of God? How would one function if one did not know the possibility of joy in suffering? How could one move forward without the hope of heaven?

There are some truths that mean nothing to a person who is gasping for existential air. When tears seem to flow continuously in your life, the nuances of the Trinity or the particulars of a certain end-times theory do nothing to comfort. However, other biblical concepts can walk a person back off the metaphorical or literal ledge when jumping seems so reasonable and appealing.

One night I sat down and wrote down all of these comforting theological principles as a personal creed. I began to realize that the Lord had embedded these individual truths in my heart that collectively constructed a narrative under which I could live during my Worst. This narrative gave me hope.

This Book

This book is my attempt to share my narrative of hope with you. One can view theological concepts as academic, arcane doctrine. Theology can seem so dry and lifeless at times. But theology breathes and becomes more than just information in a confession or textbook when it becomes the story of your life and when it constitutes bread in a desert.

The gospel is not just an evangelistic principle; it is a message that gets you out of bed in the morning. The sovereignty of God is not some debatable proposition; it is the assurance that your child's death is not a meaningless accident. Grace is not simply a word in a hymn; it's the very thing you rely on when you are so bereaved that you cannot imagine living another day. Faith is not just a cliché term for religion; it is the thing that picks you up off the carpet where you have been crying for over an hour.

My intent is that God's Word will offer you the most essential thing you need in the face of your Worst—*hope*. Hope is difficult to define until you are starving for it.

Hope is the substance that assures you that life is worth living when you simply cannot find a reason to make it to the next day. Hope is that expectation that maybe things will be better down the road. Hope is what tells you that—no matter how bad it seems—redemption is possible. Hope is that little light at the end of the tunnel that suggests that all of this misery is temporary when you're desperate for patience. Hope is the voice that says, "Don't do it," when suicide seems like a legitimate option.

In reality, all hope flows out of the person of Jesus Christ. Doctrinal truth offers no value whatsoever if it does not connect us to the heart of the precious Healer and Redeemer. This book is worthless if it does not elicit trust in and worship of the true and great Savior, Jesus Christ.

The first section, "The Initial Shock," includes what I consider the pivotal truths you need in the moments of trauma when your Worst enters your life: grace, gospel, resurrection, and faith. The second section, "The New Normal," contains theological concepts you need as the initial shock wears off and living with your Worst becomes a daily challenge: empathy, providence, doubt, presence, and sin. The final section, "The Long Haul," discusses important doctrines that help you persevere meaningfully and hopefully when you consider living the rest of your life with the wound that the Worst has inflicted upon you: joy, service, heaven. At the end of each chapter is one component of the narrative of hope, all of which are listed in their entirety at the end of this book.

To the person for whom life's buzz saw has not yet come, I intend this book to prepare you for the dark night, which no human being can elude. To the person dwelling in the gutter of misery, I hope this book grants you comfort and companionship. To the non-Christian, I pray you can see the unrivaled hope that Christianity offers.

Regardless of who you are, this book has been written for one purpose: that you may have hope.

Section 1

THE INITIAL SHOCK

Therefore the LORD waits to be gracious to you, and therefore he exalts himself to show mercy to you.

Isaiah 30:18

1

Grace

As a pastor, I frequently find myself walking into the vortex of tragedies. Being at the hospital when someone has died or entering a family's home hours after tragic news constitutes one of the great privileges and challenges of pastoral ministry.

When I walk down a corridor toward an ICU room or pace through the grass to a front door, the same anxiety always arises over this question: *What do I say?*

What do you say to a mother who has just lost her son? What do you say to a boy whose father has finally lost his battle with cancer? What do you say to parents whose child has been crippled in a car wreck? Is there really any sufficient word in such shock and darkness?

The nervousness in these situations has diminished (if not disappeared) for me since my son died. I now know the most daunting question that one faces in the immediate aftermath of tragedy.

Having left the hospital after doctors pronounced Cam dead, Lauren and I sat in Cam's room on Cam's bed, our eyes flooding with tears and our minds dizzy with disorientation. Eighteen hours earlier I had played on this bed with my son. One hour ago I saw his lifeless body on a gurney.

With our heads shaking, we repeated a question that expressed confusion, powerlessness, despair, and sorrow.

What are we going to do? Where do we go from here?

I repeated the question to a point that I felt like a zombie in a trance. We felt wholly incapable of putting one step in front of another. Who has any concept or wisdom for how to navigate tragedy? These fields of shock and sorrow are utterly unchartered for most people. Nobody ever taught a Sunday school lesson about the first steps immediately following a tragedy. Nothing can prepare you practically to answer the question, "What are we going to do? Where do I go from here?"

Furthermore, an existential boulder instantly lands on your back. You hardly can breathe with the shock of the current pain, and unfortunately, hundreds of decisions, responsibilities, and trials begin to mount.

When will the funeral be? Cremation or burial? Do you have life insurance? Can you talk to the police investigator? Have you seen the hospital bill? What will we do with his clothes?

One can only feel paralyzed with the overwhelming weight of your Worst.

For one woman, the challenge of coping with the loss of one twin in pregnancy would have been enough. Finding out that the surviving child had severe hearing loss added another level of stress and lament. One month after this diagnosis, her father died in a car accident. The wreck also seriously injured her mother. This woman had to plan her father's funeral while attending to her wounded mother. Her father owned a business that she had to manage and prepare to sell. (Yes, making payroll, canceling appointments, and filing taxes while also running to the hospital.) In addition, a criminal investigation focused on the drunk driver who hit her parents. All in the span of a year: the loss of a child, the loss of a father, the discovery of a child's disability while caring for kids, a wounded mother, and a business.

At ground zero, in the hours following the realization that she and her husband had lost a baby *in utero*, this woman never could have known that this tragedy constituted only the tip of the iceberg of burdensome, painful challenges ahead. Surely she would have collapsed and folded in despair if she could see the cumulative pressure and sorrow beyond those awful, initial hours. Surely we all would collapse and fold if God presented to us all of the trials and pains that the future holds.

Right out of college, I struggled with some health issues that required me to resign from a job. As I tried to put together a plan for a next step, I met with an older man from my church over coffee. Rather than putting the pen to the paper for a game plan on moving forward, he told me his story.

And in his story, I learned the simple, helpful answer to the most daunting question we face in the wake of tragedy.

He explained that his wife had a medical condition where she would fall into a debilitating depression for four to eight days every month. She literally could not care for herself during that monthly episode, to the extent that he would have to take off of work until his bride was restored to health.

Given how much this man's wife totally depended on him, she often would spiral into a panic when she wondered how she would survive if her husband were to die. Who would care for their kids? Who would provide for and serve her during her monthly depression episode? How could their family function? The fear of such an event paralyzed her.

This gentleman said that he offered her the same word of comfort each month. He explained that the reason she could not conceive of survival is because she was not in that situation: he was still alive. He said that God only gives us the grace for the situations to which we are called. He reassured his wife that if something ever happened to him, then God would give her the grace for *that very trial*. His wife would have vision, wisdom, and ability for that challenge because God would give her the grace she would need.

He called the concept *provisional grace*.

In my season of grief, I identified in many ways with the Israelites' journey in the book of Exodus. After the Lord released his people from bondage in Egypt and led them through the parted Red Sea, they awakened to a stark situation: they were in the desert with no food. The people began to grumble, demonstrating that their attitude toward God was not trusting (Ex. 16:2). They complained that it would have been better for them to remain in slavery in Egypt, where at least they had food, than to face certain starvation in the desert (Ex. 16:3).

Let's be honest: Do you blame the Israelites? Would you, like me, be wondering, *What have we gotten ourselves into?* They were refugees standing in a foreign, lifeless desert. They had no infrastructure for sustenance and no real direction. Numerous enemies posed a military threat, and they had no army for defense.

They still lived with the question: *What are we going to do? Where do we go from here?* The concern of basic survival existed.

God responded to their grumbling by making a promise that he would provide day by day and night by night. Each day, bread—called "manna"—fell from the sky and nourished the people (Ex. 16:4–5). In a place where there was absolutely no food and where the Israelites had no ability to provide for themselves, God's provisional grace in the form of manna met their need.

Furthermore, the Israelites had no direction in this unfamiliar land. The Lord provided a cloud by day and fire by night in the sky to guide and direct them. God supplied grace to sustain and lead the Israelites forward in their plight.

In the initial moments of your Worst, envisioning yourself as a pilgrim following God in the desert may be the wisest perspective you can embrace. You, like the Israelites, have embarked on a new journey into unchartered territory. You have left behind familiar places of security. The land around you lacks any sources of life and nourishment. You have been reduced to struggling for basic survival. Worst of all, in this barren place, you have few (if any) internal resources to aid yourself. Continuing on without miraculous means is impossible.

In the Gospel of John, Jesus declared, "I am the living bread that came down from heaven" (John 6:51). The Jewish audience to whom Jesus spoke would make no mistake about his analogy. He likened himself to the manna of the desert during the exodus.

Jesus made a provocative and clear statement with this proclamation. He said that the world is a desert with no sustenance. Furthermore, he positioned himself as the only nourishment on offer for the soul. He framed himself as the ultimate source of help for the weary heart.

In our Worst we must learn to ask constantly for God's help. We must look to Jesus, the manna who constantly falls upon us.

We must turn our eyes to Christ, the cloud and fire in the sky that leads us forward.

In order to seek God's grace, we must remember the gospel. Even if our Worst is the making of our own mistakes, the Lord desires to show mercy. Isaiah proclaimed to the Israelites, at a time of their greatest failure, "The LORD *longs* to be gracious to you; therefore, he will rise up to show you compassion" (Isa. 30:18 NIV). Notice the passion behind God's desire to extend grace to the humble who ask him for help.

God *wants* to be asked for grace. God *wants* to support you.[1]

Paul wrote to the Philippians, "My God will supply *every need of yours* according to his riches in glory in Christ Jesus" (Phil. 4:19). He does not say "some" needs but "every" need. He does not say it is because you got your act together. It is because Jesus, through the cross, has enabled God the Father to supply generously to those in need who ask for help.

As Lauren and I sat on Cam's bed in those first horrible hours of our Worst, thinking about the utterly miserable and seemingly impossible road ahead, I began to give myself the same advice I had heard right out of college. I said the only thing I honestly could say to Lauren: "All we need is grace for today. That's all we need."

And so we asked God for sufficient grace, and the Lord made it rain.

Roadside Grace

When I visit people immediately after tragedies, I tell them that they need to rely on God's help every step of the way; they simply cannot survive on their own strength. In addition, I offer a critical qualifier that came to me the week of Cam's death.

In the first hours after Cam died, I remembered a couple, Angel and Hunter, with whom I attended church in my early twenties. Their son, Lawson, went in for a relatively safe surgery at three months of age and simply never came out of it. I hardly knew this couple, but recalled wondering how in the world they were functioning in the year after their child's death. I observed them from afar and was amazed that they were still breathing. I moved to another church a year after their son passed away, but when I saw them in public from time to time over the next ten years, I remembered them as "those brave people who lost a child and survived."

Now Lauren and I were in similar shoes and struggling to conceive of how we would make it through life. This couple became a monument of hope to me. I really wanted to connect with them and seek their counsel.

Two days after Cam's funeral, as I pushed my daughter's stroller through our neighborhood, I saw a Chevy SUV cautiously slow down. As I made eye contact with the driver, I realized it was Angel. She recognized me too and stopped the car.

Even though we did not know each other formally, I wondered if maybe she had stopped by our house. Word about Cam seemed to travel fast in Birmingham, and perhaps she wanted to reach out to us. We lived in totally separate areas of town at the time—there would have been no reason at all for her to be in our townhouse complex on the other side of the city. Or so I thought.

In reality, our meeting was purely providential. At the perfect point in time and space, I was outside on a walk just as Angel was leaving a relative's house, driving on the same road we were walking. Angel represented manna, and then she became a cloud in the sky.

In that brief conversation, Angel offered the best words I heard along the journey. She told me to focus on the day, or even just the hour. She said that, in the morning, I might need to ask God for the grace to make it to lunchtime. In the afternoon, ask for the grace to make it to dinner. At night, ask for the grace to make it to bedtime. At bedtime, ask for the grace to sleep. And the next day, do it all over again.

The "grace for this hour" mentality, which emerged from this instrumental conversation, served as a foundation for our lives in the early stages of our grief.

Jesus provided similar wisdom in the Sermon on the Mount. He addressed the anxieties that people experience when they ask, "What shall we eat? What shall we drink? What shall we wear?" In essence, Jesus tackled the basic survival question of the Worst: "What are we going to do? Where do we go from here?"

Christ first reassures his followers of his constant care for them. He rhetorically asks if the birds, the lilies, or the grass of the fields worry about what they will eat, drink, or wear. Jesus affirms that God abundantly supplies for these creatures; he then asks how much more will the Lord graciously provide for his beloved children.

Jesus ends this lesson with a strict order: "Therefore do not be anxious about tomorrow, for tomorrow will be anxious for itself. Sufficient for the day is its own trouble" (Matt. 6:34). Christ calls us to a "grace for this hour" discipline. He tells us to repent from worrying about tomorrow, because we simply cannot handle tomorrow. With his help, we can only bear the difficulties of today.

When Jesus instructed the disciples on prayer through the Lord's Prayer, he called them to ask for "daily bread" (Matt.

6:11). Not for weekly or annual bread or "enough for retirement." He called them to focus on daily provision.

In order to survive your Worst, you must heed this admonition of Christ. When you find your mind wandering to the concerns of tomorrow, next month, or next year, you must repent and remind yourself, "I am only called to today. God has given me grace for today, not for tomorrow. Stay focused on the present."

God says in Psalm 119:105 that "[his] word is a lamp to [our] feet." Notice, this is not a flashlight or a spotlight; it is simply a lamp for our feet. Just enough light for what is immediately before us. This means that he intends for his Word to guide us for the next step. Not for the month or the year. Just the next step.

An alcoholic friend of mine once told me the story of an Alcoholics Anonymous old-timer who opened up about his mentality for sobriety. He admitted that if he ever found himself thinking about having a long streak of sobriety or planning on making it through the whole month without drinking, he knew he would relapse. He said, "When I'm not focused on sobriety for today and today alone, then I know I'm finished."

Each day and every week, Lauren and I had to make impossible journeys where only God's grace could sustain us. Writing an obituary, returning to Cam's school, walking by his Sunday school room, navigating genetics testing, boxing clothes—all of these were miserable, unbearable challenges. More so than these unique trials, just proceeding through the daily misery and sadness of grief was the greatest difficulty for which we needed God's help. You too probably have similar challenges—birthdays, anniversaries, holidays, recovery, etc.—where the Lord has sustained you, and you certainly have trials that loom in the future.

Life after Cam's death became a depressing journey through a melancholy desert of sadness. Each day, though, at just the right time, God would provide sustenance for the soul to carry us to the next hour. This "bread" may have looked like a meal provided, a text message with Scripture, an invitation for dinner with friends, some news about the birth of a friend's baby, a free pass to the local pool, a poignant letter, the empathetic tears of a neighbor, night-nurses, a friend sleeping on our daughter's floor, or simply a beautiful day. Regardless of the form, the help came from heaven, and it carried us through dry, lifeless territory.

Grace in Your Worst Nightmare

Life is utterly brutal in the season of your Worst. Repeatedly you will come to the conclusion that you simply will not make it. God calls us to very short-term thinking. Jesus tells us to remove tomorrow from consideration and to trust him solely for today (Matt. 6:34).

When you start to think about managing your suffering beyond this very moment, you will feel overwhelmed and depressed. By looking so far down the road, you are assuming a role that God claims. You cannot handle such a burden. Focus on trusting God for the grace of this very hour.

Remember that God is on your side. He is for you. His love for you is more than a tepid fondness. His love is a passionate, intense, self-sacrificing affection that fills his heart. It is the love of a proud father holding his beloved baby for the first time.

Furthermore, God's love moves him to offer help to sustain you in the desert. As you may sadly find, you may look for help in all kinds of places—busyness, liquor, vacations, etc.—and nothing in the world comforts your soul in a lasting, satisfactory manner. Only the grace of God can meet your desperate need in this season of darkness.

Given how horrific your circumstances may be during this period, you may react to this talk of God's love and grace as nonsense. Surely God hates me if such misery consumes my life? Rather than giving me help, my experience says that God has hung me out to dry! These feelings are fully understandable in times of suffering.

The life and death of Jesus is the greatest reassurance of these promises of God's love and help. Jesus descended from his throne in heaven and lived as a disenfranchised, oppressed, poor person, all in the pursuit of your heart. He laid down his life on the cross to provide the only satisfactory help for destitute sinners. He was separated from God the Father to the point of hell, so that you never have to feel alienated from the Lord.

The face of Jesus and the torture of the cross tell you that God is on your side. They say that he adores you. They say that he will do whatever it takes—no matter to what extent he must go—to give you the help you need. Remember that he was providing grace for you before you were even born. He did this at a time when we were sinners, actual enemies of God, as the apostle Paul says in Romans 5:10.

As you encounter challenges and repeatedly ask the question, *What are we going to do? Where do we go from here?* you know exactly what to do: Trust your Lord Jesus for his grace for this hour. Just for this hour.

The Narrative of Hope

My need is so deep; I am desperate for help. God longs to be gracious to me. He rises up to show me compassion.

He has called me to focus only on this hour, only on this day. The Lord deeply loves me. He is on my side. Out of this love comes his burning desire to help me. I can call on him, and he will give me just the grace I need for this hour of darkness. He will supply the grace for the next step. The life, death, and resurrection of Jesus assure me that God cares for me and that he will go to the greatest extent to meet my needs.

I am the resurrection and the life. Whoever believes in me, though he die, yet shall he live, and everyone who lives and believes in me shall never die.

John 11:25–26

2

Gospel

Many people say there is no wrong way to grieve. Every person mourns differently, and to try to prescribe a formula that fits all is foolish. There is one horribly wrong way to grieve, however, a way that will ruin a person's heart.

The 1980 Academy Award–winning movie *Ordinary People* depicts the disintegration of a family as a mother struggles to come to terms with her son's death. She attempts to carry on with life as if nothing happened, while the rest of her family suffers, copes, and adjusts.

The mother cannot acknowledge her resentment toward her surviving son. She cannot discuss her other son's drowning or mention his name. She cannot emotionally engage with her husband about their grief.

In the climactic scene of the movie, when her husband tries to compel her to talk about their loss, her solution is to "get away" for a weekend in order to have some fun. She thinks the absence of a vacation in her life is the problem, rather than the absence of their child.

The mother, whose family ultimately falls apart, engages in the one deadly sin of grief: she fails to face reality.

This temptation to avoid reality entices many people in suffering. Some people hide in addictions. They seek escape from their anguish through alcohol, painkillers, or pornography.

Others flee through busyness. They think that if they can just distract themselves through an overbooked schedule, then they can outrun their pain.

For some who have lost children—or even those whose youngest child simply goes to college—they try to keep the child's room exactly as it always was when he or she was there. They preserve the room, almost like a crime scene, as they resist moving furniture, pillows, or stuffed animals in an effort to pretend that nothing has changed.

In all of these cases, people work earnestly to fight off reality. They attempt to build a dam that will stand between them and the steady current of pain that follows a tragedy or loss. But ultimately the waters rise and rise, and the dam eventually breaks, and the person either struggles to breathe or simply drowns.

One's only hope of healing and redemption in suffering requires facing reality. One must emerge from denial.

But this is easier said than done.

How does a person bear reality when they have had stillborn triplets? How does one drive by a hospital when it is the place where a loved one endured an excruciating and losing battle with cancer? How does one discuss the trauma of a fatal car wreck?

Yet there is no option. In the wake of your Worst, if you fail to face reality, you will deaden your soul. If you shut yourself off from the pain, you will lock out joy. If you refuse to enter the reality of your suffering, you will not be able to enter into the blessings of life. Your heart will become hardened and closed and unhealed. Distance will develop in all of your relationships, both human and divine.

However, facing the realities of tragedy without the hope of the Christian gospel will crush a person.

Inhaling the Stench

Our season of grief included many, many miserable micro-journeys. We routinely had to enter locations with painful memories.

The Barnes and Noble store where we played with trains and ate cookies. The nursery at church. The Home Depot store where we once did a builders' workshop. Cam's school at Briarwood Presbyterian Church. These places evoked so much pain because we could see Cam's absence so saliently.

The worst of these painful entries involved entering his bedroom for the first time after his passing. It was the place that he loved so much, and the place where Lauren had found Cam not breathing.

Other than Christ's final entry into Jerusalem, no story in Scripture depicts a courageous entry quite as powerfully as Jesus raising Lazarus in John 11. Lazarus was a man from Bethany who became seriously ill. His sisters sent word to Jesus to notify him that their brother could die at any moment. They knew that Jesus had the power to heal him.

But Jesus delayed. He waited.

Jesus dismissed the claim, saying that Lazarus's sickness would "not lead to death," but that this whole scare was occurring for "the glory of God" (John 11:4). After two days,

Jesus declared that the time had come to travel to Judea to see Lazarus. The disciples protested, knowing that the authorities around Bethany were stalking Jesus, looking for his blood. His opponents wanted to stone him. Jesus's friends knew that a trip to Bethany was practically a suicide mission.

Jesus was not concerned by the danger. He marched forward into the difficulty. He knew that Lazarus had died, but Jesus had a vision of redemption in the village.

When Jesus arrived in Bethany, Mary ran out to him and fell at his feet. She lamented, "Lord, if you had been here, my brother would not have died" (John 11:32). Jesus replied by asking her to show him Lazarus's grave. With this recognition, Jesus wept. He didn't sniffle or get choked up and shed a few tears. Jesus bawled.

Perhaps he lamented for his suffering friends. Maybe he cried knowing that a comrade had been buried. Likely both.

Certainly Jesus also lamented over the reality of the deepest sting of the fall—death. Furthermore, Christ probably shed tears on his own account as he foresaw the death and grave that he himself would have to face for the salvation of the world.

Regardless, the story could have ended here. Jesus and his friends could have mourned the loss of Lazarus and gone on with their lives. But Jesus took a bold, messy step. Against the protest of his confused companions, Jesus walked to the tomb and had the stone rolled away. He stared at Lazarus's cold body. Jesus confronted the stench of death, of a corpse that had decayed for three days.

And then Christ called Lazarus, bandages and all, to new life. He raised him from the dead, and Lazarus walked out of the tomb. Without Jesus inhaling the stench and staring death in the face, no resurrection would have occurred.

To a much smaller degree and on a far smaller scale, that first entrance back into our home after Cam had passed away was our journey to Bethany. This was our moment when we had to walk to the tomb. This was the time where we had to roll away the stone, smell the stench, see the damage, and cry the tears.

The gospel is what enabled us to walk into Cam's bedroom. The gospel is the announcement of the good news that Jesus has defeated sin and death through his life, death, and resurrection. Evil and death tried to beat Jesus on the cross, but Christ took them down. He owned them. He conquered death to an extent that the apostle Paul taunts it when he says, "O death, where is your sting?" (1 Cor. 15:55).

Furthermore, as a product of Jesus's victory over death, Christ reigns as King. He sits on his throne, and with the Father and the Holy Spirit, Jesus orchestrates the redemption of the entire universe.

We could face the truth of our loss because the ultimate reality is that Jesus and life have the last word in our son's life and in our family's story.

Facing reality is utterly impossible—completely impossible—unless on the other side of that tomb is certain confidence of resurrection. We knew that Cam's story would not be the same as that of Lazarus. He would not be revived in the flesh before our eyes. But we did know that Cam was every bit as redeemed and resurrected. Through his faith in Jesus, Cam had been buried with Christ in baptism and raised with Christ in resurrection. We knew that he was in heaven and that he would walk this earth again on the last day. We knew that God could redeem our shattered lives.

This knowledge was neither verbalized nor articulated as we entered his room, but the same "Spirit of him who raised Jesus from the dead" also dwelled in us. We knew that "he who raised Christ Jesus from the dead" would also "give life to our mortal bodies" (Rom. 8:11). On our personal "Good Friday," we could see in the background of our own miniature cross the hopeful image of a future "Easter Sunday" where we could walk out of our tomb of misery as healed people.

As painful and horrific as our lives would be for years and years to come, the confidence of resurrection power provided the seed for us to open the door to our house and to walk directly into Cam's room. We cried and we cried, but we also prayed that the Lord would turn our child's room into an empty tomb, a symbol of victory and redemption, just like the grave that Christ conquered and left behind.

The Gospel Hinges on Christ's Performance

As grief proceeded, I made progress in coming to terms with our fate, but there still were pockets of denial that existed in my mind. I discovered that barriers to acceptance of reality had been erected in my psyche. They shielded me from the dark reality in a gentle way. To take on all of the pain and fully grasp the magnitude of Cam's death in one swallow would be a lethal dose. Still, I did not know the barriers existed until the harrowing moments when they fell.

For the first six months after Cam died, we changed nothing about his room. The pillows, stuffed animals, monogrammed quilts, fireman apparel, John Deere hats, and nighttime books all lay static in the room. Everything remained the same.

Then four months after Cam passed away, we learned that we were unexpectedly pregnant. A new child would be coming into our home, and the room must change. As we talked about moving Cam's bed and installing a crib, I lost it. Uncontrollable sobbing ensued.

A barrier was collapsing.

I think that, in my heart, I believed that if the room remained the same, maybe this meant that my little boy was coming home. Maybe his death was a dream. Maybe tomorrow he would show up at the front door wearing his Home Depot apron and yellow hardhat. And then we would play Legos and eat hotdogs and bathe and head to his room for pajamas.

And maybe when we entered his room, I would pick him up to hug him, and show him all of his books and toys and clothes and blankets. And I would say to him, "Look, Buddy. I knew you were coming home. Everything is the same. We kept it just like this for you because we knew you were on your way!" And we would hug and snuggle, and things would be happy again like they were in the past.

Perhaps I could maintain this hope by keeping his room exactly the same. My mind knew this was false, but my heart had not advanced.

The prospect of moving his bed crushed me.

It was an admission. It was conceding that my hope was a fantasy. It was accepting reality: Cam was not coming home.

Cam had died. He had been buried. Life would never be the same again.

This falling barrier was not a one-time occurrence. When we moved to a new home over two years after Cam's death, I faced the same problems with denial that I experienced in the early months of grief.

I felt so frustrated because I had tried to take all the right steps to advance through the season of mourning.

I wanted to be done with sadness.

But here I was, two-and-a-half years in, and clearly, deep in my heart, I still had a strong presence of denial. I still hoped that maybe Cam was coming home. I wanted to probe deep into my heart and eradicate the false hopes and expunge the pain, but I was utterly powerless to do so.

I finally had to resign to the most basic element of the gospel: salvation depends on Christ's performance, not mine. There in the life of Jesus is God living perfectly for sinners, because our attempts are futile. There on the cross is Christ absorbing God's wrath, because man cannot bear it. There in his resurrection is God's Son rising for sinners, because we are incapable of reviving ourselves.

The hope of the gospel focuses entirely on the perfect and gracious performance of Jesus. The glory of the gospel becomes even more radiant when we suffer, because we become so much more aware of our impotence to rise from the agony. We accept that only by God's grace and power can we emerge from the darkness.

You can try your hardest to unearth the false beliefs of your heart or to heal the pain, but, in truth, only God can accomplish these things. When you are in deep agony, you want to drop-kick any misguided heretic who says, "Just make a choice to be happy." If we could "just be happy," we would. If we could fully come to terms with reality by completing a workbook, we would, right?

In our seasons of the Worst, the most calming step we can take is to not only accept how limited our abilities are, but also remember how immensely gracious and powerful God remains. Christ's performance in his life, death, and resurrection provides the foundation for his work to heal now.

Healing from your Worst is a long journey. In many cases, the broken glass of your Worst may pop up years down the road.

In his first letter to the Corinthians, Paul refers to the gospel "by which you are being saved" (15:2). He connects Christ's performance in the past to the Corinthians' redemption in the present. This retrospective rhythm of looking to the past—looking to the cross—must become the dynamic of your life. And take heart; in the same way that the Holy Spirit probed deep in your soul to purify you from all unrighteousness, God will search the recesses of your heart to correct the false notions that hold you back in your grief. In the same way that Jesus knew and absorbed every ounce of your sin on the cross, he will probe all of your pain in order to heal it in his time.

Not as a result of your effort, but entirely through his.

Living under a Redemptive Narrative

I can remember one of the first thoughts that came to mind after the doctors declared that Cam was officially dead: *I never thought I was going to be "that person."*

I remember the first week of junior high, a classmate was hit by a car right in front of the middle school and broke his leg. He spent the first semester in a wheelchair. For the next six years, I didn't really know his name; I just remembered him as "the kid in middle school who got hit by a car."

With our tragedy, I feared that my wife and I would be identified at the grocery store or at the Little League fields a decade down the road as "that couple whose son died in his sleep." Even more so, I worried that our loss would become the lens through which *we* defined *our* lives. In essence, I feared that the narrative of my life had changed, and now tragedy determined the story under which I lived.

In his letter to the Colossians, Paul attends much effort to reminding his audience of the true narrative of their lives. While scholars are not completely certain about the specific problem that had arisen in this church, this epistle suggests that the members were being convinced that they needed to engage in ascetic practices and religious rituals to mature spiritually and to ward off evil spirits. Paul counters this heresy by reminding them of the implications of the gospel.

Paul tells the Colossians that the Father "has qualified you to share in the inheritance of the saints in light" (Col. 1:12). He writes that Christ "has delivered us from the domain of darkness and transferred us to the kingdom of his beloved Son, in whom we have redemption, the forgiveness of sins" (vv. 13–14). He adds that "you, who once were alienated and hostile in mind, doing evil deeds, he has now reconciled in his body of flesh by his death, in order to present you holy and blameless and above reproach before him" (vv. 21–22). He asserts that Christ is working "to reconcile to himself all things, whether on earth or in heaven, making peace by the blood of his cross" (v. 20).

In effect, Paul is saying to the Colossians, "You have lost your way. You are living under a false narrative. Why would you engage in asceticism and rituals when the living Christ dwells in you and claims your sanctification as *his* hope and purpose? Why are you fearful when Christ has defeated death? Why do you operate as if you're on your own when Jesus has moved you out of darkness and into his glorious kingdom?"

Paul intended to draw the Colossians back into the true, overarching narrative of their lives. Christ's performance—not their performance—dictated the terms of their lives. God's work to redeem all things in heaven and on earth always constitutes the definitive theme of the story.

When you encounter your Worst, the temptation arises to recast the narrative of your life. You may re-identify yourself as the woman who got the DUI, or the man who was fired for looking at porn at work, or the woman who had six miscarriages, or the man who has been diagnosed with cancer.

You fear that you will emerge from your Worst defined by the shame of your sin.

Or you may reformulate your story in terms of sadness and pain. Because you lost a child, or experienced a divorce, or killed someone in a car accident, you will never be happy again. Or even worse, you are never *allowed* to be happy again.

In all of these cases, we must remember that our stories fall under Christ's story of redemption. Your life is but a chapter in God's greater narrative of restoring the world. Your Worst is merely a chapter in your own story. If we allow God to write our stories and to carry us through the season of darkness and despair, he will ensure that redemption constitutes the central progression of our stories.

With this encouragement that our stories fall within Christ's narrative comes a grim caveat. Those united with Christ will suffer like Christ. Jesus's story was one of great hope and redemption, but it is also one of agony and anguish. Thus, our story will inherently include a similar arc. The hope of the gospel in our hearts does not necessarily protect us from the physical and emotional pain from which the Father did not spare Christ. Nevertheless, consider what glory we bring to God and what encouragement we offer to others when we walk redemptively in our story. We give people a real glimpse of the resurrection.

The Gospel in Your Worst Nightmare

You may be at the beginning of, or in the middle of, your long, hard walk into a valley of darkness in the wake of your worst nightmare. You may be preparing for your season of tragedy down the road. As painful as it is, you have no choice but to walk into the darkness and to lean into the pain. The worst thing you can do is to bury your head in the sand and avoid reality.

In spite of the promises of redemption, you will continue to experience pain in the wake of your Worst. Until we reach heaven, we still dwell amid the effects of the fall.

Therefore, you must continue to return to the gospel over and over. You must look at the cross and see Jesus's performance on your behalf. You must stare at the empty tomb and see Jesus promising you redemption.

As waves of pain pound against your heart, you may start to sink back into despair, feeling as if your sadness will drown you. You again must turn your mind to the gospel. The cross and resurrection will serve to stabilize you as a fixed event that reassures you that God can and will redeem your life. Nothing is impossible for God.

As you look to the cross, remind yourself that your story falls within Christ's story. And know that the end of Christ's story is redemption. God is leading you out of the tomb and making it an empty one. There is hope.

The Narrative of Hope

> The road ahead of me is long and painful, but Christ has defeated sin and death through the cross. I can face reality and make this journey, because on the other side of the cross is the resurrection. In the same way that Christ rose from the dead, so too can my life emerge from the darkness

into light. The gospel tells me that I cannot redeem myself; only Christ can heal and free my heart. My only hope is to trust him to do so. My tragedy has not disrupted the narrative of my life. My story remains God's story, and that is a story of redemption.

And if Christ has not been raised, your faith is futile and you are still in your sins. Then those also who have fallen asleep in Christ have perished. If in Christ we have hope in this life only, we are of all people most to be pitied.

But in fact Christ has been raised from the dead.

1 Corinthians 15:17–20

3

Resurrection

"*Lauren, Christ is risen from the dead.*" There lies the most significant sentence of my life. It was the first sentence I uttered when my wife delivered the crushing news that my son had died.

Why was this my first reaction to the worst news I had ever received? Understanding and unpacking this sentence makes "Resurrection" the most significant chapter in this book. It's the key sentence underlying your hope and survival in the midst of your Worst. In fact, it's the sentence on which the entire world hinges.

A convincing voice will relentlessly work to persuade you to despair in response to your Worst. The voice follows you around, hoping to see you wither and regress. That resurrection sentence was my weapon against the voice.

Tragedy and suffering have a way of raising all our beliefs and notions into a powerfully bright light. Waters of despair and fear accumulate on the fringe of our hearts. The dam that prevents them from crashing in and flooding our hearts is truth.

Knowing that the promises of God are absolutely true, that they are inviolable laws of the universe, is utterly essential in your Worst. If heaven is just wishful thinking, then it's meaningless when someone dies. If the sovereignty of God is a theory, then you have no assurance that he remains in control when life appears to be falling apart. If Jesus is just a person rather than "the way, and the truth, and the life" (John 14:6), as he proclaimed, then he has limited help to offer because he is not much better than you or me.

Christianity, as seen in the Bible, presents itself as the absolute spiritual truth of the universe. People in modern culture often resist viewing matters of faith and spirituality in absolute terms. They view faith in an individual and subjective manner.

Some Christians and non-Christians espouse their faith because it feels right. Perhaps they have had a number of joyful or peaceful experiences deriving from their spiritual practices that have led them to affirm a particular path as the best one for them. Life for the most part has been good; therefore, they believe God is good.

Others take a more pragmatic approach. Their religion "works for them." It provides a certain level of utility in coping with stress, offering moral guidance, and finding meaning in life. They would not necessarily recommend their faith to everyone, but for their purposes, it gets the job done.

Many, particularly young people, engage in "pick and choose" Christianity. Robert Wuthnow refers to this process as "tinkering," whereby people "piece together [their] thoughts about religion and [their] interests in spirituality from the materials at hand."[2] They procure truths, beliefs, and practices from a variety of sources and assimilate them into a self-made faith of sorts. Sometimes they may adopt certain moral and theological aspects of their faith (perhaps Christianity) while declining other parts that do not align with their preferences.

The problem people encounter under a subjective and individual approach to faith is that they deny that their views contain absolute truth. They do not believe that the truth of their religious beliefs extends beyond their own life and underlies the entire universe.

Why does the nature of one's faith matter? Why am I getting so philosophical in a book meant to offer hope and comfort to sufferers? Here is why: If your faith is not absolutely true and based on God's Word, then, I promise, it will not amount to a handful of gravel on the day of your Worst. You will not have an answer to combat the voice, which will persistently taunt you.

When you choose your child's burial clothes, you do not *feel* as if God is good. When you carry your child's coffin to a grave, a pragmatic faith will not "work for you." I promise. And when you drive home from the cemetery, ingesting the reality that you never will see your child again on this earth, the sobriety and magnitude of those moments will expose a "tinkered" faith for what it is—a self-crafted religion with no real answers. It will offer a level of comfort similar to Santa Claus and the Easter Bunny.

Tragedy will pulverize a subjective, individually crafted, emotion-based faith.

If you find yourself in this place—finding your faith crumbling and not sustaining you—as you read these pages, I do have good news. There is an answer to the voice of despair.

A major shift occurred in my life during my junior year of college. I stopped following Christ because it worked and felt good. I started following him because I believed the worldview portrayed in Scripture was actually true.

A relatively mild disappointment in college overwhelmed my emotion-based, pragmatic faith. I thought that if I faithfully obeyed God, then I would get what I wanted. When what I wanted didn't develop my junior year, I was crushed and angry. Very angry.

In a reckless interstate car ride I repeatedly screamed the question, "Why do I even believe this stuff? Why do I even trust God if things don't work out the way I want them to?" I did not have an answer.

After several hours of dangerous driving and bitter lamenting, God answered my question by giving me this simple realization: *Because it's true.*

In those moments I remembered the resurrection. I now had an answer to the voice.

In that traumatic phone call on the morning of Cam's death, I essentially communicated to Lauren that all the tenets of the Christian faith that we deeply cherished remained reliable and firm in spite of the tragedy that had entered our lives. God's character—his love and sovereignty and goodness and holiness and justice and wisdom and kindness—remained intact. The promises of the gospel—our salvation, God's presence, and our heavenly hope—had not been altered.

Although we experienced significant disorientation as our minds and lives were spinning chaotically in those initial moments, God planted seeds of hope by giving us the answer to that voice of despair.

Why the Resurrection?

You may be sensing a bit of disconnection. In the previous section, I said that my initial statement regarded the resurrection of

Christ; yet I dedicated the entire section to the objective truth of Christianity. How are the two interrelated?

The apostolic writings point to the bodily resurrection of Christ as the basis for the truth of Christianity. Not creation. Not the ethical superiority of Jesus. Not the perfect preservation of scriptural manuscripts. The entire faith lives and dies on an empty tomb. If a person wants to overhaul Christianity, don't point to evolution and science. Don't make philosophical arguments. Don't critique the moral and ethical positions of the faith. Disprove the resurrection and the entire Christian ship will sink.

The apostle Paul said to the Corinthians that if Christ did not rise from the dead, then their faith was "futile" and "vain" (1 Cor. 15:14, 17).

For this reason, Paul took great effort to verify for the Corinthians that Jesus indeed rose from the dead. Keep in mind that Paul was writing to a skeptical audience, much like a modern audience today.[3] Many Greeks possessed a leery attitude toward supernatural claims such as that of a corpse coming back to life after dwelling in a grave for three days. Paul, who spent a great deal of time at the church of Corinth, knew how much these church members might struggle to accept such a miraculous claim.

As a result, Paul appealed to eyewitness testimony of credible witnesses. He says that Christ appeared to Peter ("Cephas"), one of the most known leaders in the early church. In a sense, Paul offered him as a celebrity witness to the resurrection, as the members of the Corinthian church likely would have known of and respected Peter. This appeal would equate to saying that a famous, internationally recognized Christian leader saw Jesus raised from the dead.

Paul then writes that Jesus appeared to the disciples and to "all the apostles" (1 Cor. 15:5, 7). Once again, the disciples and apostles would have been well-known, credible witnesses to the Christians in Corinth. Furthermore, given the leadership that the apostles and disciples provided for the early church, it is likely Paul uses these allusions as interpersonal footnotes. In other words, a Corinthian Christian probably had access to or a relationship with an apostle whom they could ask to verify the bodily resurrection of Christ. Paul and other apostles visited and invested in the Corinthian church, and he essentially offers the opportunity for the members to verify his claim of a bodily resurrection with one of them.

Paul also tells them that Jesus appeared to more than five hundred people at one time, many of whom were still alive when he was writing, who could function as eyewitnesses. Paul shows that Christ did not simply reveal himself post-resurrection to his inner circle. In doing so, he dispels the notion that Jesus's closest friends conspired to manufacture a myth. He demonstrates that, just as Christ's death was public for all the world to see, so was his resurrection. Jesus appeared to a crowd greater than five hundred people.

Most of all, Paul offers himself as the most unlikely, but perhaps most credible, witness of the resurrection. He reminds the Corinthians that he persecuted the Christian church. Paul's encounter with the risen Christ was so real and so profound that it effectuated a radical conversion in his life, to the point that this former opponent of Christianity became one of Jesus's greatest all-time advocates and apologists.

He essentially says, "Guys, you know me. You know my story. We spent months together. If there's anyone who didn't want to believe this claim, it was I, but I saw Jesus risen with my own two eyes. If you don't believe the testimony of those other people, at least trust me!"

Christianity had exploded, and the entire basis and testimony for this world-changing movement was the witness and proclamation of the bodily resurrection of Jesus.

I know it may seem odd that in a book largely committed to comforting sufferers, I am writing about this truth of Christ's resurrection in such an academic, cerebral manner. As a person who has attended my own son's funeral, I can tell you that everything you believe will be thrown into question when the Worst enters your life. Everything you feel and experience will tell you that none of these promising messages of Christianity are true.

The voice of despair speaks so convincingly in our saddest moments.

God certainly isn't good, and if by chance he's good, there's still no way that he loves me. If any of it were true, then why am I so miserable and unhappy?

You must have a weapon to counter the voice, which wants to defeat you.

In my life as a Christian, whenever I have had doubts about whether this Christianity business is just something convenient that I use to cope with life, or if it is a product of my cultural context, I end up back at the empty tomb.

If Christ rose from the dead, then the theological dominoes start to fall. Jesus of Nazareth claimed to be God—having power over life and death—and he predicted his own death and resurrection. If his prediction of rising from the dead comes true, then surely he is God. And if this man proclaims a message of good news and redemption, then certainly this declaration must be the word of God. If this man, who is God, attests to and believes in the veracity of all of Scripture, then the Bible must be from the Lord. And if the Bible is, in fact, the Word of the Lord, then the message of God's love for sinners and Christ's redemption of the whole world is reality. All of the promises of hope and comfort and healing become relevant.

Pastor and author Rick Warren summed it up in this manner after his son, Matthew, passed away:

> I have a very clear recognition that the truth of the Gospel is either true or it's not and if it's not true then we just need to forget it all, go home, call it a farce, call it a fairytale and go home. But if it's true, if Jesus did raise from the dead, then that means that Jesus is alive today, and Matthew is alive today, and we'll be alive someday when we leave this life, when these bodies die.[4]

Here's the good news: this grand, cosmic message filters down from a universal scale and applies to none other than you. Yes, you and your life. No matter how dark or destitute your situation may be. No matter how tragic your loss. No matter how grievous your sin. No matter how dire and desperate your circumstances.

All the promises and comforts—the presence of God, the possibility of joy, the empathy of a suffering God, the hope of heaven, the promises of the redemption of the world, the availability of grace, the gospel—apply to your story. The promises of the gospel become something you can bank on. They comprise a narrative under which you can live and thrive and hope.

They're not wishful fantasies; they are your life.

If I cannot assert that Christianity is absolutely true throughout the universe, then I cannot confidently make any of these hopeful promises to you in this book. Since I do believe that

Christ rose from the dead, I can look you in the eyes through the ink on the page and say whole heartedly, "There is hope. You will get through your Worst."

The First Steps in the Journey

On November 11, 2013, my life changed forever. Disorientation. *Cam? What? Dead? No. No. Not real. How do you know? Not breathing? Stiff? Not real.* Walked to car. Like a robot. Called friend. *Get away from the kids. The worst news. What? Yes. What? Yes, he's dead.* Mechanically rose out of driver's seat. Walked to passenger seat. *Where am I? Is this hell? Hospital?* Bright light. A fog, a daze. A spinning head. Pulled up to a hospital. *How did I get here? "Sir, you can't park here." My kid is dead inside; you can have the car.*

After I received the phone call from Lauren that she'd found Cam not breathing and with no pulse my friend Walker, drove me to the children's hospital where the ambulance had taken my child.

A terrifying first step awaited me as I sat with Lauren in a family conference room, knowing that an awful announcement was forthcoming. Around the corner came a young ER doctor and a pair of nurses who confirmed that, indeed, Cam had passed away. My worst nightmare was now officially my life.

With this pronouncement came a moment all parents hope to never encounter: Lauren and I had to go into the hospital resuscitation room to say goodbye to our child for the last time. It was the worst twenty-yard walk I ever could imagine. Two older clergy mentors walked us to the threshold of the room.

As I turned the corner, I saw the white-blonde curly locks and boyish frame. The body of my precious son was lying lifeless on the hospital bed.

Could this be real?

Was this really happening?

Surely, that was not my child?

But it was.

It was Cam.

For ten minutes I held, caressed, and kissed my sweet little boy's body. I told him how much I loved him and what a special boy he was. I ran my fingers through his soft, thick hair. Weeping on my knees on that frigid tile floor by the bed, I told my son goodbye.

Then, it was as if the Lord came up from behind me, placed his hands under my shoulders, and lifted me from the ground. Amid my despair, a rush of the Spirit struck through my heart, and I felt an unrehearsed utterance coming from my mouth.

With my hand on my little boy's chest, I declared to the doctors and nurses in the room, "If Christ isn't risen, then I am completely screwed right now. I have no hope, and I am finished. But, you know what? Christ is risen from the dead. It's true. This little boy is in heaven, and I will see him again. This situation utterly sucks, but I'm going to make it, because Christ really is risen and God really is good. I have hope."

The resurrection isn't just a fact; it's the dynamic of our lives. Before Paul offers his justification for the resurrection in 1 Corinthians 15, he reminds the Corinthians of the gospel "by which you are being saved" (v. 2). As I said before, not *were* saved or *will be* saved, but presently "are being saved."

Your resurrection began when Christ rose from the grave. It became *your* resurrection when you received Christ as your Savior. Now resurrection is a continuous (and sometimes invisible) work that God is doing in your life. In some moments you are aware of it, and in others not.

God is a resurrection God. His routine work is that of reviving people and redeeming lives from all kinds of dark places.

You are a resurrected person.

You have a life of resurrection.

Resurrection in Your Worst Nightmare

In the season of your worst nightmare, so many people, including me, will tell you of the promises of God. They will say that he is with you, he will help you, he cries with you, he will heal you, etc. At times, it is comforting. At other times, you want to throw your hands up in the air and say, "Give me a break!" Life can be so miserable in the valley, and it's hard to believe all of this supposed good news.

I have to tell you that I sincerely believe that the Christian story, which promises you hope, healing, and redemption, is true. Fortunately, this belief is not something I have internally mustered up. There is a claim in time and space—the cross and resurrection of Christ. You can look to this claim of a living, loving God and see it as verifiable. The resurrection supplies you with the definitive counter-answer to that enemy voice.

This historic fact also ensures that the hopeful promises of the gospel do not simply dwell in abstraction and theory. They are not just nice ideas. They are the laws of the spiritual realm that undergird your life. The resurrection bridges the spiritual truth to your heart, mind, and life.

Christ has risen from the grave and defeated sin and death. You may feel utterly buried in misery, but the resurrection offers you the hope of redemption. Nothing is hopeless. No chapter closed. No shame or trauma is beyond God's restoration. No wound beyond his healing power. If God can raise a man from death, he can certainly resurrect your life from the ashes.

The Narrative of Hope

Christ claimed that he was God. He claimed that he could forgive sins. He claimed that he would redeem the world. He rose from the dead and proved his promises to be true. God's promises of redemption are not wishful fantasies. They are real, relevant, and powerful promises based on an event in history. If God has the ability to raise Jesus from the dead, then he can redeem all of my suffering and misery. The life of my Worst is buried with Christ in death and will be raised with him in resurrection power.

I waited patiently for the LORD;
    he inclined to me and heard my cry.
He drew me up from the pit of destruction,
    out of the miry bog,
and set my feet upon a rock,
    making my steps secure.

Psalm 40:1–2

4

Faith

In the days following a sudden loss, sufferers may be tempted to think, *I'm doing fine under the circumstances. This isn't as bad as I expected.* People fill your house. Plans for the funeral are made. Flowers come through the door. Letters fill the mailbox. These supports and distractions shield a person from the reality of what has happened.

Furthermore, psychological shock prevents one from processing the magnitude and sting of a sudden death. You know it's bad, but you don't know the extent of the damage.

After the people leave the house, the funeral has concluded, and the letters slow down, reality begins to settle. For some, it's a slow process, while for others, their Worst strikes them with a blunt-force blow.

As an analytical person, I classified the different ways that I cried after Cam died. There were "confusion cries" of "*Why, God? Why?*" There were "sweet cries" where I remembered my precious child and shed tears of gratitude that, even for a short time, I got to enjoy this adorable little person. There were "sad cries" in the everyday, melancholy moments.

Then came the "Mike Tyson cries," which came rarely but unforgettably.

For those who never followed heavyweight boxing in the 1980s and 1990s, Mike Tyson was the most ferocious, dominant boxer who ever lived. People watching Tyson fight did not wonder who would win—they simply prayed that Tyson's opponent would not die.

In his first heavyweight championship victory, Tyson landed a cold left hook to the face of Trevor Berbick, sending him to the mat. Berbick pitifully tried to stand up, but his disorientation and inability to rise constituted one of the most humiliating scenes in heavyweight championship history. Berbick stumbled around and simply could not stand.

So was my experience when my first "Mike Tyson cry" seized me. Plenty of tears had been shed in the first days of mourning, but shock, busyness, and a crowd of people prevented brutal reality from setting in. Then, late one afternoon, I was home alone at a time when our baby, Mary Matthews, normally napped in her room and the raucous sounds of "little boy" *usually* filled the rest of the house.

It was the day after Cam's funeral.

It was quiet.

So quiet.

Reality punched me in the face and then in the gut. This was final. It was over. Never in my life on earth would I see, touch, or hear Cam again. My son was dead. His sounds, his voice, his presence—they were gone. I heard and saw their absence for the first time that afternoon.

I started to wail with an intensity that I never knew existed, a lament that made my stomach contract. I fell to the ground and simply could not stop crying and could not move. I dinstinctly remember the sensation of having carpet fibers in my teeth because my face was buried in the carpet as I sobbed.

I felt like Trevor Berbick, lying on the mat with no hope of standing up. The fallen world had delivered a blow that left me staggering. As I lay on the mat, a looming beast promised to crush me again if I dared to stand up. Standing up meant facing the punishing punches once again. At least Trevor Berbick could tap out and exit the ring in that moment; I perceived that my own version of Mike Tyson would stalk me for the rest of my life.

How was I going to live? How could I make it through the rest of life in this kind of pain? And, more immediately, how in the world was I ever going to get off the carpet?

Faith as Rescue

When people think about faith in the Bible, many immediately associate the verse John 3:16: "For God so loved the world, that he gave his only Son, that whoever *believes* in him should not perish but have eternal life."

Very often people misunderstand "believing" in Christian salvation as our part of the bargain. Jesus did his part on the cross. We do our part by believing. It's a partnership of sorts.

Certainly all sinners bear a responsibility to trust in the grace of Jesus for salvation, but if they conceive of faith as a joint venture, they misunderstand the nature of saving faith.

Faith in Christianity constitutes far more than "getting by with a little help from your friend (Jesus)." It's more than "Jesus is my co-pilot." It is actually an all-out, full-on, 100 percent rescue.

When I lay prostrate on the floor after my first visitation from Mike Tyson, the position of the speaker in Psalm 40 came to mind. He proclaims,

> I waited patiently for the Lord;
> he inclined to me and heard my cry.
> He drew me up from the pit of destruction,
> out of the miry bog. (Ps. 40:1–2)

The speaker depicts his entrapment in misery. He resides in a nasty, dim place—a muddy bog. Imagine being knee deep in the mud of the swamps of Louisiana, amidst the putrid smell of stagnant water. Feel the discomfort of wet slime in your shoes. Everything around you looks the same.

Not only does the speaker dwell in a muddy swamp, this bog sits at the bottom of a "pit of destruction," which some commentators describe as a place like hell. It's as if he stands in a bog with tall, unscalable walls surrounding him. The image is clear—the speaker is trapped in darkness and misery.

He cannot escape.

The 1986 story of "Baby Jessica" captures the extent of our inability to escape. An eighteen-month-old baby named Jessica McClure fell twenty-two feet into a narrow well with casing only eighteen inches wide. Given the small width and great depth of the well, Jessica had no hope beyond extraordinary means for rescue. Furthermore, she was a baby—they could not throw her a rope and cry, "Just hold on tight while we pull!"

After the shock wears off and the Worst strikes, you may know the feeling of being stuck in a pit. Everyone in grief has his or her encounter with Mike Tyson. Everyone falls to the bottom of the well like Baby Jessica.

Paralyzed by a feeling of despair, it is easy to feel incapable of climbing out of such a dark, emotional mire.

The speaker in Psalm 40 proclaims that God "*drew me up* from the pit, . . . out of the miry bog." There was no climbing out of a muddy pit. There was no carrying on, as the band Fun suggests, "if you're lost and all alone."[5] There was no "just press on," as some well-meaning moron told me two days after Cam died. There was no tossing a life-rope or a ladder.

For Baby Jessica, dozens of engineers worked continuously over two days to form a tunnel. Then they traveled down and carried the helpless baby out.

That is also the image of God's rescue in Psalm 40. God climbs into the mess, picks up the desperate soul, and carries him to solid ground.

My only hope was for God to scoop me into his arms and to lift me off the mat of misery. My only hope was the rescue of God.

The true gospel informs a proper view of faith. God didn't come to earth in the person of Jesus Christ because we needed a little help. He came because we, his people, were drowning in turbulent waters in our sin. Jesus collects us from a dismal condition.

As any trained lifeguard will tell you, the natural reaction of those who are actively drowning is to fight off their rescuer. Lifeguards are trained to approach those at risk from behind, to prevent them from grabbing and forcing the lifeguard under water too.

Faith—both in our initial salvation and in our deliverance from the pit of despair—involves a desperate cry to God to rescue us. It means fighting off the temptation to resist our Deliverer or to white-knuckle our way out.

The faith that enables you to stand up from the mat begins with relinquishing all hope of self-rescue and fully trusting Christ to pick you up.

Consider the stories of the Israelites wedged between the water and the formidable Egyptian army, or Joseph cast in the pit, or Daniel in the lion's den. In these stories, God redeems people from inescapable danger and certain death. *We may think that these stories represent exceptional circumstances, but the salvation of every single sinner is no less miraculous than God delivering Shadrach, Meshach, and Abednego from the fiery furnace.* The apostle Paul captures this reality well in his second letter to Timothy:

> The Lord will rescue me from every evil deed and bring me safely into his heavenly kingdom. To him be the glory forever and ever. (2 Tim. 4:18)

If you conceive of faith as a partnership or joint venture between you and God, then you will find yourself in a desperate place in those moments where your hope and strength are totally depleted. With a partnership mentality, you mistakenly stand on equal or similar footing as God. The danger comes when the Worst knocks you down and you find yourself with no internal resources at all to find your feet. It is in these times that you must first remember Christian faith as allowing God to rescue you. You must fully surrender and completely depend on Christ. You must acknowledge your dire need of him and expectantly rely on his faithful redemption.

Does this mean that you have no part in standing up? No, certainly times exist where you must move; you must take the right steps forward. Simultaneously, faith as rescue constitutes the foundation of being able to take any steps at all.

The good news is that Jesus desires to deliver you. Christ is always willing and near.

Seeing Your Rescuer

Understanding faith as rescue is an important foundation for hope in your Worst. Faith means little, however, unless you can personally trust and see the Rescuer.

Very often, Christians define faith with the terms provided in Hebrews 11:1: "Now faith is the assurance of things hoped for, the conviction of *things not seen.*" What could be a better definition than one that comes straight from the Word of God?

I'll be honest, this definition made little sense to me until I entered my Worst. The verse felt like a collection of religious jargon. My understanding of what faith means in Hebrews 11:1 finally awakened because of the phrase "things not seen."

Tragedy makes "seeing" a fearful challenge in daily life. While you may conceptually accept that God is a deliverer, all of the visual wreckage and debris that surrounds your life after a tragedy undermines the notion of God's goodness. For most people, images of their Worst pervade their daily lives, creating frequent challenges to faith.

The United States military deploys a bomb known as the MOAB (Mother of All Bombs) to destroy bunkers deep beneath the ground. This explosive, which weighs over 21,000 pounds, does not have such a destructive force because of a giant inferno. Instead, the invisible concussion of the bomb's detonation can disable technology, damage bunkers, and kill people within an expansive radius.

Like the MOAB, the Worst has similar unseen force in the world immediately around you. All of a sudden, mundane places within your home, your local park, or your church become painful symbols. They have not physically changed at all, but the invisible destruction of your Worst has damaged and tainted these places and objects.

The aisles of the grocery store, where you simply shopped for food each day, become the place where your deceased child used to hang on the shopping cart. The lake house, where you spent summers with your husband, becomes a location to be avoided at all costs. The stairs to the nursery at church, where you used to drop off your child for morning worship, become a dark corridor.

A woman once told me that for fifteen years she never went down the neighborhood road where her sister died in a car accident. A father who lost a son told me that he did not go upstairs in his house for two years because the sight of his son's bedroom overwhelmed him. A woman who miscarried several children told me that receiving medical bills of any sort in the mail created substantial anxiety because of the memories of paying such bills after her failed pregnancies.

For many, their house becomes a place of traumatic recollection. The pictures, the clothes in the closet, the swing in the backyard, the bedding, the crib, the armchair, the little booties—they all become objects capable of eliciting pain in your heart and challenging your trust in God's goodness.

I still drive five minutes out of my way to avoid passing the entrance of the children's hospital emergency room where Cam was pronounced dead. In the first year after Cam died, the sight of parks, Barnes & Noble, Home Depot, tractors, and fire trucks generated a tight feeling of sadness and trepidation in my chest.

The Rescuer stands as the critical bridge between you and your rescue. However, people cannot hope to be rescued if they cannot trust the person to whom they must cry.

The "things seen" can create difficult barriers between the Rescuer and you. When the images surrounding you constantly oppress you—they constantly remind you of your Worst—then faith becomes even more challenging.

The audience to whom John wrote the book of Revelation faced this same challenge. Often people wrongly view Revelation as apocalyptic prophecy written apart from any historical context. In reality, this book communicated important truths and images to seven late-first-century congregations in dire hardship.

The seven churches in modern-day western Turkey, addressed in the opening of Revelation, experienced intense persecution. The Roman world around them rejected and mocked their faith. Some Christians lost their jobs and their families. Government officials threw many in prison. In at least one of these seven communities, people were killed for pledging allegiance to Jesus.

Imagine their struggle. They were among the very first Christians. They had taken radical risks in deciding to follow Christ. Certainly, many of them felt burned as they saw and experienced such darkness around them.

Consider the images of their life. Look at the chaos, harshness, affliction, violence, and costs that resulted from their decision to follow Jesus. Their experience seemed to contradict the promises of hope, comfort, and abundant life that flowed from making Jesus their King.

To encourage and exhort these persecuted Christians, God gave them a look behind the curtain and into the spiritual realm through Revelation. While they saw chaos in their community, God provided an image of the glorious, sovereign King reigning from his throne. While they saw rampant injustice, God portrayed scenes of holy, divine vindication that would come to their oppressors. While they saw the fallen world at its worst, God painted a portrait of the beautiful, majestic new heavens and new earth that they would one day enjoy.

Like the seven churches of Revelation, the images of our Worst challenge our faith in God. If we base our views of God on the circumstances around us, then tragedy will wreck our ability to trust him when the Worst comes our way. Among the pain and disappointment of our lives, we will find little evidence that God is the one whom we can call to for our rescue.

A wise older mentor of mine once defined faith as "proper response to what God has revealed." Indeed, while you cry out to God to rescue you, you must also look to the things "unseen" to build your confidence that God is the one who can heal, strengthen, and deliver.

The true source for revelation of God's character and his redemptive work throughout all time is his Son and the Scripture. We should not look to our circumstances to assess whether or not we can call to him for rescue; we look to his Son and to the Bible.

In the same way that God gave the persecuted Christians in western Turkey the prophecy of Revelation as assurance of his sovereignty, love, and goodness, he has given believers his Son and all of Scripture as our peek behind the curtain. When we look to his Word, we see the true character of God. We see the true, redemptive narrative under which we live. We see who truly remains on the throne: the *holy, holy, holy* triune God.

We must acknowledge that the painful images around us are real. The crib is empty. The clothes in the closet are unused. The scar on your chest is not an illusion. Those images truly exist.

The Word of God is the "truer truth." It is the true representation of the Rescuer.

In 2 Kings, Elisha and his servant faced a faith struggle similar to the churches in Revelation. Elisha had continued to snuff out the king of Syria's plans to attack the Israelites. As a result, the Syrian king sent an army to surround the city of Dothan to take out Elisha. When the servant of Elisha woke up and saw the city completely besieged, he cried in despair, "Alas, my master! What shall we do?" (2 Kings 6:15).

The servant saw undeniable truth. He saw the mighty Syrian army and a hopeless military situation. However, Elisha called for God to enlighten his servant to the "truer truth." Elisha petitioned God, "O Lord, please open his eyes that he may see" (2 Kings 6:17). In response, the Lord provided a vision of a massive spiritual army of fiery chariots and horses standing on the mountain with Elisha. Through spiritual means, God saved his people. God provided the servant with a look behind the curtain, which enabled him to trust God for his rescue and move forward.

Notice that Elisha had to ask God to help his servant see the "things unseen." We cannot force ourselves to see the "truer truth." We need the Holy Spirit in conjunction with God's Word to help us see behind the curtain into the spiritual realm. As author and counselor Gordon Bals once told me, "Sometimes we need to trust God for the faith to trust God."

The closest my faith came to cracking was about five weeks after Cam died. In addition to his dying, a bombshell had gone off in our extended network of relationships. Then, in the same week, I also had discovered that an old friend had cancer. In the midst of all this sad news, we had a teething baby who screamed all night for a week.

After being up from 12:30 a.m. to 3:30 a.m. with no success in quelling the baby's nonstop cries, I snapped. I put the baby in her crib, went out to the living room, and proceeded to pound a pillow against the couch psychotically for ten minutes.

I screamed angrily, "God, haven't we had our fair share? As if our kid dying isn't enough!"

My wife swiftly rebuked me. She knew my pain and frustration, but she also knew that I was relating to God based on "things seen" rather than "things unseen." She started citing Scripture, reminding me that God was our only hope and our only rock. She then made me call my pastor friend.

My friend, Murray, walked me to the curtain and peeled it back. He compassionately spoke scriptural truth to me until I had settled down and God, through his Word, had restored my faith.

One of the make-or-break factors in whether people will find hope in their Worst involves the amount of their exposure to Scripture. God's Word transcends and trumps the painful symbols surrounding you. His truth provides the images of hope, which counter the images of pain and despair.

You must constantly cry out to God for rescue. God's Word enables you to trust him for deliverance by reminding you of his goodness and trustworthiness. God's Word enables you to see your Rescuer, standing above the painful images and waiting to embrace you.

Faith in Your Worst Nightmare

When you enter the season of your Worst, you feel trapped. You feel stuck. You cannot conceive of escaping the misery and sadness that defines your mood. You cannot imagine that a long cry will ever end. You don't know how you will get out of bed.

More than anything, you cannot imagine functionally living a normal life, given the cloud of darkness over you.

When you feel as if you are responsible for climbing out of the pit in your own strength and being the author of your own redemption, you become utterly overwhelmed. You cannot conceive of emerging from the darkness.

You must understand that in the darkness of your Worst, God—and only God—can redeem you. Faith is not a partnership; it is total dependence on the Lord. God does not call you to climb out of the "miry bog" (Ps. 40:2). He calls you to cry out for mercy and to trust him to rescue you. He can and will deliver you.

The many painful images around you present a major challenge in trusting Christ. The "things seen" constantly suggest to you, "God is not good. He's abandoned you. You cannot trust him. You're on your own." God's Word and the Holy Spirit are your allies in seeing your Rescuer and trusting him for deliverance. They will help you see the truer truth that indeed the Lord is kind and good.

You can trust your blessed Rescuer.

The Narrative of Hope

Even though I dwell in darkness and anguish, God can rescue me. I am not called to redeem myself. I am called to shift my burden to Jesus and to trust him to deliver me from this pain and despair. God can do it, and I can rely on him to be my Redeemer.

Section 2

THE NEW NORMAL

For we do not have a high priest who is unable to sympathize with our weaknesses, but one who in every respect has been tempted as we are, yet without sin. Let us then with confidence draw near to the throne of grace, that we may receive mercy and find grace to help in time of need.

Hebrews 4:15–16

5

Empathy

When two sets of parents, who both have lost children, realize that they share this common tragedy, they often say, "So you're in our most thankless fraternity too." They frequently use this language of being in the "club" or "fraternity" to describe the common wound that creates an instant bond and mutual understanding.

Five months after Cam died, Lauren and I traveled to New York for a conference. After purchasing my favorite macarons in the world at *Laduré*, we walked past the Frick Museum on our way to a bench in Central Park.

We randomly chose a bench facing the skyline south of the park, featuring a view of Trump Tower and The Plaza. We settled in with hopes of a light moment spent debating the merits of lemon macarons compared to the chocolate and caramel macarons.

While we reclined and indulged, I saw that our leisure time instantly would become heavy when my eyes caught sight of the shining bronze plaque on our bench.

Lauren and I had sat down on a bench honoring a child. Friends had dedicated this space to a young lady named Ashley Meade O'Connell. I looked a little closer at the memorial and noticed that Ashley had lived from 1993 to 1999, a short life of six years.

I cried.

I cried and cried and cried.

The memory hit so close to home. With my face buried in my now wet-hands, a lament that cried "Children are not meant to die" flowed through my heart. As I gazed at the New York City skyline through the branches of towering trees, I wondered about Ashley's story. I wept for her parents. Her passing was fifteen years prior, but I knew that her mom and dad must still be mourning somewhere with a suffering as towering as the skyscrapers before me. I wondered what the pain of the first year must have been like for them, as I was in the midst of it myself. I pondered what their tears must have been like at her funeral and how intensely they still must miss her. I wondered if they visited her grave and told stories about her to keep her memory alive. I imagined what Ashley's birthday and the anniversary of her death must be like for them fifteen years later.

In ways, I already knew these strangers.

In classic technology-age fashion, I googled this child's name and found an entry on a memorial site dedicated to the stories of children who have passed away due to cancer. There I read this beautiful entry:

> Ashley Meade O'Connell
> December 10, 1993–July 29, 1999
> Neuroblastoma
> Ashley was our only child. She was an incredible child who always brightened our days. She will always be loved and remembered.

The word "always" in the script told me that these were "my people." A person who has lost a child clings to the deep hope that their child will always be remembered. Never ever forgotten.

I felt connected to this couple although I didn't even know their names. I felt that our tragic bond meant we could understand each other within minutes of meeting, in a manner that people spared this misfortune simply could not. We could connect instantly at a deep level because of a common, sorrowful history. As crazy as it seems, I wanted to be friends with these people whom I did not know, simply because two numbers on a plaque were far too close together.

The lonely day comes when people stop asking, "How are you doing?" The season arrives when people quit talking about the one you lost. When you reach these moments, a desperate need to be understood develops, and you long for conversations and relationships with those in the fraternity.

There are fraternities of all kinds of suffering in which only the members can identify with one another. For people who have lost a spouse or who lost a parent in their childhood, the laments are different. For victims of abuse and rape, they share an anguish of which no person possibly could conceive, except other victims. For those who struggle with depression or bipolarism, a dark cloud hovers over them that only those with the same struggle can "get." Common suffering yields a camaraderie, comfort, intimacy, and respect among its fraternity members.

Support groups naturally evolve out of common plight. Women who struggle with infertility, families with alcoholic relatives, people who suffer from addiction, and widows or widowers gather weekly in communities across the world to relate their stories and to bond over their common wounds.

Lauren and I have found this to be true with other parents who have lost children. The deceptive hope that when you enter your child's room in the morning, he will be in his bed. The dread of holidays. The lamentation of putting his old clothes away. The cloudy fog into which you descend when you call his memory to mind. Avoiding certain places such as the children's hospital because you just can't handle it. The wondering about what he may have been like at age four or fourteen or twenty-four or forty-four. The random, awkward tears in public. The questioning of whether this is a bad dream or if this is real, months and even years later.

You feel as if you only can trust people at the most intimate level—you only can share the deepest lamentations of your heart with people in the fraternity.

You need the fraternity.

A Facebook Status

Waking up the first morning after Cam's death was one of the worst moments of my life. It was as if I'd been told the news for the first time all over again. It was as if an invisible messenger stood by the bed with a cold, expressionless face, saying, "Yes, it happened. It's true. Your living hell is real."

With the confirmation of our tragic reality, I decided that Lauren and I needed to announce our sorrowful news publicly through Facebook. Interestingly, at the core of my November 12, 2013, Facebook announcement stood the empathy of God:

> We are profoundly and devastatingly sad and will grieve the loss of our sweet boy for the rest of our lives. But we can live with hope, peace, and gratitude knowing that the promises of the gospel are true and knowing that Christ indeed is risen from the dead. Our God lost his Son, and so

> have we. God's Son was raised from the dead, and so was ours, all thanks be to Christ. Our precious boy knew Jesus and is with him now. Blessed be the name of the Lord. God remains good.

Foundational to my hope stood the realization that my God lost a son too. He was in our fraternity.

A bereaved father once bitterly (and reasonably) asked a clergyman who had come to visit him after his son's passing, "Where was *your* God when *my* son died?" The priest replied, "I would imagine the same place he was when *his* son died."

For any person who has lost a child, God is a friend who can share in the common experience. He is one with whom bereaved parents can have "insider" conversations that only people who have lost children "get."

In the same way that parents who have a child with a terminal illness live in dread of the day their son or daughter will inevitably pass away, God the Father lived with that same dreadful anticipation, knowing that he had sent his Son to die on the cross.

In the same way that many parents have witnessed their child pass away, God saw every second of his Son's death on the cross. He saw people put nails in his Son's hands. He saw a spear stabbed in Jesus's side.

In the same way that some parents must go to identify their child's body, God identified Jesus's beaten, lifeless body. He saw his Son's corpse.

In the same way that bereaved parents must plan and attend their child's funeral, God stood by as people put the stone on his boy's tomb. He heard the thud of the closing coffin door.

In the same way that bereaved parents experience the anguish of separation from their child, God knew this separation to the deepest degree. While my child went to heaven upon his death, God the Father experienced separation from his child, when Jesus took on the sins of the world.

The empty chair at the dinner table. Their absence at holidays. The vacated room. The unplanned weeping. God knows all of it. God is in the fraternity.

During the Lenten season, many Christians hear the song, "Were You There When They Crucified My Lord?" And the song asks, "Were you there when they nailed him to the cross?"

God was there for every second of it. God was there when his Son died at the hands of the very people he had come to save. God knows our pain better than anyone.

A Man Acquainted with Sorrow

The beauty and mystery of the Christian faith is that God is an empathetic being. Notice, I did not use the word *sympathetic* but *empathetic*. The difference is critical, as empathy comes from the ability to share an experience with another sufferer.

Author and scholar Brené Brown narrated an insightful cartoon where the artist illustrates the principle of empathy as a person climbing down a ladder into your ditch, rather than observing from above. Nothing fosters empathy like shared experience.

God communicates his empathy through the incarnation of Christ. God becomes a vulnerable person who knows the common day and traumatic sufferings of every person. In a prophetic text, Isaiah described Christ, the suffering servant, as a "man of sorrows and acquainted with grief" (Isa. 53:3). Jesus knew the pain of skinned knees, ridicule, colds, rejection, and conflict. He knew the pain of torture, public humiliation, and violence.

He is an in-the-trenches God who empathizes—not just sympathizes—with our suffering from his own firsthand experience.

Have you ever been hated? Jesus has been too.

Have you ever suffered in poverty? Jesus did too.

Have you had friends stab you in the back? Jesus did too.

Have you ever had a cousin murdered? Jesus did too.

Have you ever anguished to the point that your skin emitted blood? Jesus did too.

Have you ever been mocked? Jesus has been too.

Have you ever been beaten? Jesus has been too.

A person may rightly protest that Jesus genuinely suffered in his earthly life, but he did not know what it's like to have a miscarriage or to have cancer or to be trafficked into the sex trade. Jesus did not experience every trial.

It may serve as a comfort to remember God as a divine parent who shares in the diverse sufferings of his children. I heard it with disbelief and as theory when my mom said that a parent feels their child's pain twice as much as the child. Then I became a father and found it to be true. A mother aches more deeply over her son being bullied than the boy does. A dad seethes and laments over his daughter's broken heart more than she does. God experiences and endures every ounce of suffering that his children undergo in their lives.

Furthermore, we all are members of a collective fraternity of those who are suffering in any way in the fallen world. We all know pain, loneliness, disappointment, sorrow, and grief. Jesus, as one who took on human flesh and joined this fraternity, is with us.

The author of Hebrews encourages his audience that "we do not have a high priest who is unable to sympathize with our weaknesses, but one who in every respect has been tempted as we are, yet without sin" (Heb. 4:15). This is a theological way of saying, "God gets it." The author communicates that God understands our challenges as human beings in the fallen world.

With this reassurance, the author encourages people to "draw near to the throne of grace . . . with confidence" (Heb. 4:16). Because God in the person of Jesus Christ is a member of the general fraternity of human suffering, we can bear our heart before him. We can go to him when we need understanding. We can trust him with our pain.

I know that my Lord God wept and wailed alongside me. He was in my unique fraternity. He had walked in my unenviable shoes. In the same way that I felt connected to the parents of Ashley Meade O'Connell and wanted to know them, I also felt connected to God in a deeper way. I felt a deeper bond and knew he could understand my sorrow in a way that nobody else could.

God can understand and empathize with your sorrow better than anyone you ever will find. You can draw near to him with your sorrow.

Empathy in Your Worst Nightmare

God the Father feels your pain. He does not sit on a distant throne but enters into the trenches of suffering with you. When you weep, God weeps too. If your heart has been broken into a thousand pieces, then his heart has been broken into ten thousand pieces.

Jesus did walk the path as a fellow sufferer in the fallen world. He understands you. He understands your pain.

You can draw near to him as one who is in your special fraternity of unique suffering. You can feel safe and known in his presence.

When the crowd quits asking, Jesus continues to inquire, "How are you doing?" And when you answer, he's the one who understands your pain the best.

The Narrative of Hope

God understands my suffering. He lived as a vulnerable, afflicted human being in Jesus Christ. When I cry, he cries. When my heart breaks, his heart breaks. I can trust him as a fellow sufferer who empathizes with me.

And we know that for those who love God all things work together for good, for those who are called according to his purpose.

Romans 8:28

6

Providence

In times of tragedy and suffering, well-meaning pastors and friends frequently offer a religious word that momentarily appears helpful but proves hopeless in the end. As sufferers wrestle with how a loving, good God could allow such painful, wicked things to occur in our lives, people want to say, "God didn't have anything to do with this."

After the attacks on the World Trade Center on September 11, 2001, a pastor spoke on a radio program about how we make sense of such evil. The pastor declared that God had nothing to do with these attacks and said to listeners, "Satan is still the prince of this world."

A colleague of mine heard the same sentiment expressed at the funeral following the suicide of a middle-aged woman. The pastor spoke directly to her family from the pulpit and assured them, "You need to know that God didn't have anything to do with this."

I listened to the podcast of a parent who had tragically lost a young child through an accidental death. She said that her pastor reminded her that God is not a "grand puppeteer," sitting in heaven orchestrating all the events of the world.

But as a friend, let me sit down with you and tell you the immediately hard but ultimately hopeful truth about your Worst: God did and does have something to do with your tragedy. I know this sounds like a cruel statement, but stay with me. There is hope in the end.

There is both a *fundamental* and a *practical* reason why the notion of God's limited involvement in suffering breeds harm and hopelessness.

Let me tell you what I hear when people say, "God didn't have anything to do with this." I hear . . .

God's hands are tied.

God took his eyes off the road when your Worst occurred.

Satan is just as great, mighty, and sovereign as God.

God just isn't that powerful. He's impotent.

God is not in control.

God is weak.

None of these statements resembles the God of the Bible. The witness of Scripture testifies to a God who remains sovereign in every moment.

The Bible says that God controls the forces of nature (Ps. 147:15–18). His providence rules over plants and animals (Jonah 4:6; Matt. 10:29). He ordains random events (Prov. 16:33; Acts 1:23–26). He reigns over rulers and nations (Job 12:23–25). He controls major disasters (Lam. 3:37–38; Amos 3:6). He has power over the spiritual forces of evil (1 Sam. 16:14; Matt. 8:31–32).

If God controls all these elements of existence—all of which are far less significant to him than you, his child—then certainly he reigns in the story of your life, even in your Worst.

A story my mentor Rev. Frank Limehouse labeled as the most significant moment in his early ministry career illustrates why the sovereignty of God is so instrumental in maintaining hope during the season of your worst nightmare. Frank, as a seminary student, was shadowing a hospital chaplain when they were called to a room where a woman's son had been pronounced dead after a tragic car accident. The woman lamented over and over again, "Why did God do this to me? Why did God do this to me?"

The chaplain, trying to be helpful, inserted, "Ma'am, God didn't have anything to do with your son's death."

To this statement, the wailing yet wise woman pointedly looked the chaplain in the eyes and replied, "Don't you take away the only hope that I have."

Behind the grieving mother's remark lies the hope that the sovereignty of God enables. If God is not fully sovereign in your suffering, then you cannot trust that he is fully in control of your healing and recovery. If God's hands are tied when the Worst enters your life, then maybe his powers are also limited in helping you.

Moments will come in your Worst where it feels as if God has left the building. The scriptural word concerning the sovereignty of God assures you that even in the moments when it feels as if God has abandoned you and your plight, you can know objectively that God remains in control in those moments of fear and despair.

I have the obvious indications that God ordained Cam's death. On a Sunday afternoon, my perfectly healthy child asked me if he could go see Jesus. He asked if we could get in the car and travel to heaven. He wondered whether he would see Adam and Eve in glory. He professed faith in Christ. Eighteen hours later, my wife found him dead in his bed.

It would take an irrational level of skepticism to deny that God put those thoughts on my son's heart and to doubt that God orchestrated his expression of faith in Christ's saving grace. That these, the most beautiful moments of my time as a parent, occurred immediately before Cam's death is no coincidence. It confirms my faith in God's full control in Cam's life and death. Consequently, it also confirms my sense of confidence in God's sovereignty in my Worst.

You may not have some magical story like mine to offer you the same comfort. This is why I emphasize the objective promise of God's sovereignty in his Word. God reigns supreme when the Worst enters your story, and God reigns supreme as he works in every second to heal and restore your heart and your life.

Your Worst Is Not Meaningless

The idea that God had nothing to do with my son's death terrifies me. If I were to believe that he was not involved in Cam's death, it would shatter my entire worldview. For all of these years I would have falsely believed in a universe with higher order and purpose. I would have falsely believed that God is holding all things together and moving all moments toward an appointed end where justice and redemption ultimately prevail. I would have falsely believed that all of life had meaning.

But those beliefs would fall apart if God didn't have anything to do with Cam's death.

This false suggestion proposes that some moments have meaning and some moments do not. If God had nothing to do with my son's death, then certain pockets of life—the really awful ones in particular—are given over to chaos because the God of the universe is removed from them. In the case of my

Worst, and in the case of yours, if God is not involved, then it has no purpose.

My receiving the traumatic phone call, my holding Cam's corpse, my attending his funeral, my carrying his casket, and my weeping and weeping and weeping would all be meaningless because God had nothing to do with it.

But that is all a lie.

According to the Bible, God is sovereign. He was in control before, during, and after my Worst, and he is in control throughout yours. Consequently, your Worst has meaning. Your Worst has purpose.

In times of tragedy, people often cite Romans 8:28: "All things work together for good, for those who are called according to *his purpose*." Too often we overlook two pivotal aspects of this verse. First, we misunderstand the definition of "good." We tend to think that "good" involves prosperity, happiness, and comfort. From the context of Romans 8, however, "goodness" involves believers being conformed to the image of Christ, fruit being borne for God's glory, and God drawing his people into deeper fellowship with him. This form of "good" often comes out of deep pain, but God does "work good" in everything—both the happy and the sad.

Second, we overlook that we are called "according to *his* purpose." The purpose of God is "to unite all things in him, things in heaven and things on earth" (Eph. 1:10). We cannot always see the redemptive activity of God in either the mundane or the difficult, but God promises that every element of our lives fits into a grand, redemptive story whose significance and beauty are far greater than we conceive.

For me, I find hope in trusting that my son died because God determined before the foundation of the earth that Cam would live three years and fifty-five days. My son died for a reason: he died that people may see the beauty and majesty of Jesus Christ and that God may fully redeem and perfect the broken world. Cam's death is neither random nor meaningless. I may not necessarily see a fraction of the ways God accomplishes this, but his Word promises me that it is true.

Let me tell you the truth: *your* Worst is not random or meaningless.

God Is Not Punishing You

The level of God's control in your suffering is critically important, but it really isn't your foundational concern. A question inextricably linked to God's sovereignty constitutes the make-or-break issue.

In Isaiah, God foretells the exile of the Israelites. His people had been warned to repent from idolatry and cautioned against putting their faith in alliances with foreign countries. God warned the Israelites of the risks of provoking their aggressive enemy, the Babylonians. Alas, God's people ignored him, and they fell prey to invasion, conquest, and exportation by the Babylonians.

While he foretells the Babylonian exile, God also promises the redemption of his people. He pledges to bring them back to Israel and to forgive their sins.

In Isaiah's prophecy, God clearly states that these events will occur and that God himself will direct them. In Isaiah 46, he contrasts himself to idols, declaring,

> I am God, and there is none like me,
> declaring the end from the beginning
> and from ancient times things not yet done,
> saying, "My counsel shall stand,
> and I will accomplish all my purpose. . . ."

> I have spoken, and I will bring it to pass;
> I have purposed, and I will do it. (Isa. 46:9–11)

The invasion and exile that God ordained was not pleasant.

The Israelites experienced their worst nightmare when they were attacked and then exiled. They witnessed atrocities at the hands of the invaders. Many Israelites experienced starvation. They were removed from the land so dear to them and taken to a foreign land to live as second-class citizens while pagans tore down their sacred temple.

What makes this passage compelling is that God proclaims his sovereignty in the events before they occur. The passage is prophetic. In essence, God wants them to know before their Worst happens that he is in control of their fate. For God to predict the events and remind his people of his ordination of them suggests that he must consider his sovereignty an instrumental aspect of their ability to trust and hope in him amidst suffering.

However, an Israelite reader still enslaved in exile two centuries later—a victim of these tragedies—would find no hope in God's total control without this question being answered: *Is God good*? More specifically, *Is God good to me*?

A person with total power but with wicked character is a dictator—a Joseph Stalin, an Adolf Hitler. In Isaiah 46, God reminds his people of his goodness even more so than of his sovereignty. As the Israelites carry their idols into exile, God promises, "Even to your old age I am he, and to gray hairs I will carry you. I have made, and I will bear; I will carry and will save" (Isa. 46:4). Even as God refers to them as "you stubborn of heart," he promises, "I bring near my righteousness; it is not far off, and my salvation will not delay; I will put salvation in Zion, for Israel my glory" (Isa. 46:12–13). He demonstrates his love for them in that he will deliver and save his people whom he cherishes, even though they are rebellious and sinful.

If you believe in a sovereign God, you cannot help but feel that God is afflicting you when you are living your Worst. You cannot resist asking the question, "Why are you doing this to me?" You cannot help but feel as if you are being punished for something and God simply does not like you.

What the well-meaning but false-speaking pastor or friend is trying to do with the statement, "God didn't have anything to do with this" is preserve the goodness of God at the expense of the sovereignty of God. In that statement, there is a failure to recognize that God can remain fully in control during tragedies while still being completely good.

The best way one can reconcile God being both sovereign and good is through the cross. Was there ever a moment where God's sovereignty was more evident? The prophets predicted the slaughter of a suffering Messiah for the atonement of God's people centuries before Christ's birth (Isaiah 52–53; Daniel 9). Jesus insisted throughout his ministry that his mission would culminate on the cross. On the night before Jesus died, he asked God if the cup could pass, if his will could be altered, if he *must* die. God willed Jesus to the cross. In spite of the brutality and the pain, from before the foundation of the world, God ordained the violent death of his Son (1 Pet. 1:19–20).

At the same time, was there ever a place where the goodness of God was more magnificently on display than the cross? In the cross, God expresses his love for us to the degree that he subjects Jesus to torture and sends his own beloved Son to hell for our ransom and rescue. From the cross, God screams to each and every one of us, "I am for you!"

The cross tells us that God is not punishing us through our Worst. Everything that God could punish us for was laid on Jesus in his death.

God punished Jesus so that he never would have to punish you. Your Worst is not God taking out his frustration on you for all your shortcomings, nor is it God recreationally torturing you.

The matter of God's sovereignty and goodness invokes tension. One would be naïve and disingenuous to ignore the paradoxical nature and logical difficulty in unifying these doctrines. God opposes sin but he remains in control over the wicked, harmful decisions of people? God hates evil but he allows it to act in the world? God authors life and yet he ordains death? God detests injustice and yet he allows sinister tyrants to reign?

People possess a will and make decisions, which have consequences. Satan is a real, personal force in the universe. Nobody can (biblically) deny these facts. God did not pull the trigger when a teenager committed suicide. He did not fly the planes into the Twin Towers or lead suicide bombers to ignite explosives in a crowd. He did not encourage or approve of the drunkenness that led to a person's death. And, at the same time, God remained in control of the circumstances leading up to these moments of darkness. God remained in control during these events. He remains in control in the results of these events. God ordains the past, the present, and the future.

These paradoxes become far more confusing when they are *your* paradoxes. *God loves me but he allowed my husband to drop dead while we are raising young children? God is for me but he allowed my child to have cancer? God loves my child but he allowed her to be diagnosed with schizophrenia?*

Again, the cross is where our best comfort resides. While we wrestle with the tension and suffer in the mystery, we must keep our eyes on the cross, where we see God's beautiful glory exploding from the intersection of his sovereignty and goodness.

Providence in Your Worst Nightmare

God is in control of your life. He doesn't take his eyes off the road when your Worst occurs. He isn't taking his eyes off the road as he restores you.

You need to know that your Worst is not a meaningless accident. God has redemptive purposes for everything that enters your life. You will not see the full extent of those purposes until you get to heaven, but you can trust that the pain you are enduring is not ultimately pointless.

The most important thing for you to remember is that only God's goodness and love for you supersedes his sovereignty. The cross reassures you that even in the most painful of circumstances, God remains fully in control and fully good.

The Narrative of Hope

My trial is not a random accident. Nothing comes into my life but through God's perfect discretion. God remains in control of all circumstances. He has a hand in my painful circumstances, which means that his hand can extend to redeem my life. God is good. The evil in this world and the suffering in my circumstances do not represent his character. The perfectly kind and loving person, Jesus Christ, is the very image of the character of God. The cross reassures me of his love and sovereignty. I can trust him, knowing that he is fully good and fully in control.

And Jesus said to him, "'If you can'! All things are possible for one who believes." Immediately the father of the child cried out and said, "I believe; help my unbelief!"

Mark 9:23–25

7

Doubt

After Cam died, my interest in my hobbies, especially sports, waned. I developed a distaste for anything that I had taken too seriously before. Having experienced such a tragedy, I was disgusted with myself for having stewed for days over trivial things such as sports defeats.

My passionate interest in Alabama football declined. Before, I had read about Tide football every day; afterward, I hardly logged onto those websites. Before, I listened to sports talk radio in the car; afterward, I never did. When Alabama squandered a national championship opportunity to conclude the 2013 season, I just didn't care. A malaise of apathy had formed.

Oddly, one thing from the football season did drive me mad, and it made absolutely no sense, given my newfound indifference toward football. I found myself noticeably angry about one play that occurred in a Georgia versus Auburn game six days after Cam died.

Georgia had mounted a late-game comeback to take a one-point lead in the fourth quarter. Auburn's chances looked dismal. They faced 4th and 18 from their own 27-yard line with only 25 seconds left on the clock. Auburn's quarterback hoisted up a Hail Mary in desperation. The Auburn receiver had lost track of the pass, while two Georgia defenders were right under the ball, ready to make an interception. Instead of batting the ball down or intercepting it, however, the two defenders batted the ball up into the air. The ball changed trajectories and traveled right into the arms of the Auburn receiver. He ran it in for the winning, 73-yard touchdown. The play was so extraordinary that sports journalists dubbed it "the Miracle in Jordan-Hare."

It irked me. All my interest in college football had declined. Alabama lost to Auburn the next week, and I barely shrugged my shoulders. I didn't even bother to watch the national title game that year for the first time in thirty years, and I declined free tickets to see Alabama play in the Sugar Bowl. But the only evidence of any interest in sports involved my bitterness about one play that occurred six days after my son died. Why was it that, months and months later, I could not shake this bitter fixation?

It all came back to probabilities.

On Sunday, November 10, 2013, when my wife put my son down to sleep, there was, medically speaking, a 1 in 620,500,000 chance that he would die in his sleep on that particular night.

On Saturday, November 16, 2013, with 25 seconds left on the clock, there was a 1 in 1,000 chance that a winning touchdown would be scored on that particular play.

A sports team pulled the "football victory" lottery ticket. As a result, they won the exhilaration and glee of sports glory.

I pulled the "child's death" ticket. As a result, I won a lifetime of sorrow.

It felt so unfair.

Only 1 in 100,000 children above the age of one will die in their sleep. The ball of genetics had bounced in just the wrong direction and my son had died. In our case, there were 99,999 families on one side of the aisle, and we sat on the other aisle. Alone.

The juxtaposition of improbabilities—not the outcome of a sports game—is what was eating away at me. To be the outlier in the stakes of human tragedy ignited a sense of perplexity, anger, and doubt.

This little story captured only an ounce of the confusion I experienced, and continued to experience, during my season of grief. The first word of the lyrics of my life became "Why?"

> *Why* my child?
> *Why* my family?
> *Why* is the world so messed up?
> *Why* is life so painful?
> *Why* is a cross the way of redemption?
> *Why* not someone else?
> *Why* did you do this to me?
> *Why*, Lord, *why*?

Sometimes the questions were laments of sadness, and sometimes they were cries of anger. The moments of anger were existential and pointed toward the brokenness of the cosmos. Rage formed against an utterly twisted world flooded with pain, death, violence, injustice, hatred, despair, and confusion. Daunting doubt asks, "Why does it have to be this way?"

Doubt and the Gospel

So often, religious people criminalize doubt. They mistakenly believe that it's a sin to ask God "Why?" They act as if Christians need to bite their tongues and put on faces of resolve. Or better yet, they think that people just need to repeat Christian platitudes until the anger and confusion go away.

So many people have been spiritually abused by this "name it, claim it; doubt it, go without it" mentality. *If you can just muster up enough faith internally, then you can beat your pain and anger through spiritual effort.* You effectively heal yourself through self-engineered "faith," or so the fallacy goes.

If people live in the truth of the gospel, they should expect that human beings will live with lots of questions in their lives. In fact, a person can even demonstrate a proper level of humility and wisdom in those questions. The gospel points to our insufficiency and incapability as human beings and, therefore, points us to our need for God's grace and wisdom.

To shame doubters implies that people ought to have sufficient wisdom in and of themselves. They should be without weakness. Such shaming contradicts what the gospel clearly says about people: We are a mess. We only are healed of our weakness before God.

Proverbs states that "the fear of the LORD is the beginning of knowledge" (Prov. 1:7). A simple way of explaining that verse is knowing that *God is God, and you are not.* "The fear of the Lord" means that a person lives with a recognition that God is an all-good, all-knowing, all-holy, all-powerful, and all-wise Being. Meanwhile, we, as fallen humans, aren't that good, aren't that smart, aren't a lick holy, aren't very strong, and aren't particularly wise.

Job represents the paragon of holiness in the midst of suffering. Job, a blameless man, received an all-out onslaught from the Enemy, which first resulted in the loss of all his wealth and was followed by the death of all his children in one fatal catastrophe. As if he had not suffered enough, Job was also stricken with an irritating skin disease and sores from head to toe.

After various dialogues with his friends, Job lamented to God. He effectively asked, "What have I done to deserve this?" Job genuinely believed that he had tried to worship the Lord in his life as righteously as possible. He had avoided lust and greed and idolatry. He had cared for his servants and looked after the weak and needy. Now he sincerely requested that God give him an account for his wrongs if his sins had, in fact, provoked these calamities.

Job's deepest desire was for an answer. "Just give me an answer, Lord!" he effectively said in lamenting,

> Oh, that I had one to hear me!
> (Here is my signature! Let the Almighty answer me!)
> (Job 31:35)

We first must recognize that God identified Job as a man whom no person in the world surpassed in righteousness. Immediately after the death of his children, Job worshiped God. He pronounced that all that he had came from God and that God had the right to "give and take away." Job's lamentation, where he wailed with confusion and begged for an answer, did not constitute a break from the holy posture he had already demonstrated throughout his grief.

Too often, people look at this part of Job's story and assume that his fault lay in expressing his doubt and raising questions before the Lord. Job did have error in his heart, but the iniquity did not reside in his lamentation. The act of expressing his confusion and mourning before God was not sinful.

It is not sinful to cry out to God!

It is not sinful to express your confusion!

It is not sinful to ask God "why"!
God responded to Job with these words:

> Where were you when I laid the foundation of the earth?
>   Tell me, if you have understanding.
> Who determined its measurements—surely you know!
>   Or who stretched the line upon it?
> On what were its bases sunk,
>   or who laid its cornerstone,
> when the morning stars sang together
>   and all the sons of God shouted for joy?
>
> Or who shut in the sea with doors
>   when it burst out from the womb,
> when I made clouds its garment
>   and thick darkness its swaddling band,
> and prescribed limits for it
>   and set bars and doors,
> and said, "Thus far shall you come, and no farther,
>   and here shall your proud waves be stayed"?
>
> Have you commanded the morning since your days began,
>   and caused the dawn to know its place,
> that it might take hold of the skirts of the earth,
>   and the wicked be shaken out of it? (Job 38:4–13)

The temptation exists to view God's response to Job entirely as a scolding, sarcastic slam. God did rebuke Job, who had crossed a line. Job had assumed that God had punished him because of his sin. He sensed a potential inconsistency in God's system of justice, and he responded presumptuously. In essence, Job's flaw was that he presumed to know too much and he overestimated his ability to understand. In a sense, God's reminder of his own majesty and power pushed Job back into the correct place of mystery and doubt.

Do you hear what I am saying? I am saying that Job's sin lay in his *lack of doubt*. His sin was over-confidence. He presumed to know the mind and intentions of God in his particular situation and demonstrated arrogance inconsistent with the proper fear of the Lord.

In his rebuke, God blessed Job by bringing him back into reality. In a sense, God said to Job, "Of course you are confused and frustrated. Do you realize how complex and intricate all the details of life and existence are? Only a person with the ability to form the world and sustain all its complicated systems can comprehend the purposes behind the suffering and trials in life. You, Job, are not that person."

Kenneth Harris and August Konkel comment, "Job (unlike his friends) is not reproved for furthering folly but rather because the inferences he has drawn from wisdom have not properly reflected what he is able to know in light of what he believes to be true."[6]

In Deuteronomy, Moses writes that "the secret things belong to the LORD our God, but the things that are revealed belong to us and to our children forever, that we may do all the words of this law" (Deut. 29:29). The secret things—God's reasons, intentions, and plans in the trillions of circumstances in the world every day—are innumerable. For Job, for you, and for me, God has reasons why certain trials have entered into our lives, and we only have access to an infinitesimal fraction of his reasons.

Given the vast discrepancy between who God is compared to who we are, living in doubt and mystery often represents the most humble posture we can assume toward the Lord in our suffering. In these doubts we communicate, "God, you are God, and I am not." Honestly expressing those doubts through worshipful lamentation can be the response most consistent with what the gospel tells us about the relationship between God and man.

God's Character Is the Answer to Your Doubts

The prophet Habakkuk had a confrontation with God similar to Job's. As he looked at all the corruption among the people of Judah, he went to God and effectively asked, "Why are you allowing this to happen? How can you stand by and allow your people to desecrate your name and your Temple?" (see Hab. 1:2–4). God's answer completely defied Habakkuk's expectations. God initially said that he was "doing a work in your days that you would not believe if told" (Hab. 1:5).

I would imagine that Habakkuk got his hopes up with this promise. Maybe he wondered, "What's God going to do? Maybe everyone will repent, and we will thrive again in every way!"

Not exactly. God went on to tell the prophet that he intended to send the Babylonians—the worst people on the face of the planet in the eyes of a good Jew—to conquer his people (Hab. 1:6–11).

What? This is the "amazing" news?

Habakkuk replied with what serves as a good model for dealing with doubt before God. He asks a litany of questions.

God, aren't you good?

Aren't you pure?

Aren't you the defender of your people?

He just did not understand how the God of Israel could commit to such a plan, and he was honest about it.

After rattling off his questions and expressing his confusion, Habakkuk concluded with this bold statement:

> I will take my stand at my watchpost
> and station myself on the tower,

> and look out to see what he will say to me,
> and what I will answer concerning my complaint.
> (Hab. 2:1)

Habakkuk announced that he would stay in the conversation with God. He had honestly expressed his doubts and confusion. He had gone before the Lord. And now, he would wait for God.

He offered no pithy clichés. He did not act pious to "God's face" and then lambast God in the privacy of his home (as if that's even possible). He did not quit on God and walk away from the relationship in a defeated or victimized way.

Habakkuk told God the truth of his doubts to his face—every ounce of frustration and confusion—and then he trusted the Lord by remembering his character, waiting on him, and remaining in the relationship. He dignified his relationship with God by struggling in it.

So often, Christians hide their pain behind trite religious platitudes. "God's got a plan" or "Everything happens for a reason" or "This too shall pass." I do not criticize anyone who finds comfort in the truth of these statements. At the same time, however, when people try to tie up their pain and confusion in a tight little bow and, thereby, oversimplify the depth of their grief, they run the risk of creating distance from God and planting seeds of bitterness in their hearts. In this way, they try "be strong," when the very response to which God calls them to is weakness.

In 2 Corinthians, Paul lamented over "a thorn in his flesh" that plagued him. It was a trial and difficulty that he asked God to remove, and still it remained. Paul did not understand why the Lord would not deliver him from it. Paul concludes this lamentation by expressing his contentment in the mystery and by saying, "When I am weak, then I am strong" (2 Cor. 12:10).

People need to run straight to God humbly with their doubt and confusion. They need a "pro-honesty" relationship with him. Rather than suppressing their true feelings before the Lord, people need to pour out their hearts before the Lord with a reverent spirit.

The Archbishop of Canterbury, Justin Welby, lost his daughter Joanna in a car crash in 1983. He spoke to this need for honesty with God in a 2015 sermon where he reflected on his own struggle with doubt:

> Time goes by. And I remember that, and that sense sometimes of "What's it all about? What's it all for?" We were Christians, and sometimes people turn away from God and sometimes they turn to God, and like the psalmist they say, "Where were you? Where are you?" It's in the Psalms. Tough words, bitter words, of anger with God. Much better said than suppressed.[7]

Understanding the difference between doubt and unbelief serves as a remedy in this tension. Habakkuk demonstrated his doubt and faith simultaneously. He didn't "get God" in these moments, but he trusted him. That he "waited for the Lord" demonstrated that he expected goodness to flow from his Lord, no matter how painful and disappointing the actual circumstances might be.

If Habakkuk were living in doubt and unbelief, he would have forsaken God. He would have walked away from his petitions and lamentations because he did not trust in the Lord's goodness. Unbelief involves thinking that God stands against us and that his goodness is questionable. Unbelief leads us away from wrestling with God and leaves us, instead, wrestling with our flesh within our minds. Faithful doubt means trusting in God's goodness while expressing our pain and confusion.

For a person to express doubt rather than to use trite Christian platitudes exhibits humble faith. It asserts that "God is big enough for my doubts. He's forgiving enough for my lack of faith. He's powerful enough to turn my trepidation into peace." Such laments demonstrate an admission of weakness, acknowledging that mortals just cannot figure out why life is so difficult. Admission of weakness and the need for God and his wisdom constitutes the birthplace of healing.

Habakkuk's dialogue with God ends with these words of comfort and assurance:

> Though the fig tree should not blossom,
> nor fruit be on the vines,
> the produce of the olive fail
> and the fields yield no food,
> the flock be cut off from the fold
> and there be no herd in the stalls,
> yet I will rejoice in the LORD;
> I will take joy in the God of my salvation.
> GOD, the Lord, is my strength;
> he makes my feet like the deer's;
> he makes me tread on my high places.
> (Hab. 3:17–19)

His circumstances had not changed at all. He got no more positive news about his future. Still, Habakkuk had hope and joy.

When you know and trust in the goodness of God amid your doubts, this same joy and hope is offered to you. Our feelings and circumstances always change; God's character remains the same forever.

Mystery

In all three of the stories presented in this chapter—Job's, Habakkuk's, and mine—resides one common result: God never answers the question of *why*. God told Job that he is the great and mighty God. He told Habakkuk that he would do something impressive. Still, they were left in mystery.

For me, I have asked God thousands of questions and have never received an answer. I have accepted that I never will understand why my little boy died at the age of three. For the rest of my life, I will live with that mystery.

Too often people think that our peace will come from an answer to *why*. In reality, peace and comfort flow from the question of *who*.

My comfort comes in what has been revealed to me about the character of God through his Word and through his Son, Jesus, the very image of the living God. The explanation of Cam's death remains a "secret thing" to me, and belongs to God. What has been revealed—what belongs to me, a child of the King—is God's Word. Out of his Word flows the promise of his goodness, wisdom, and holiness.

God has told me that he is gracious and compassionate (Isa. 30:18). He has told me that he is perfect, upright, and just (Deut. 32:4). He is wise and brilliant (Job 12:13). He is good (Ps. 34:8). He is all-powerful (Rev. 7:12). He forgives (1 John 1:9). He makes all things work for good for those who have been called by him and love him (Rom. 8:28). He is making all things new (Rev. 21:5). He has proven all these attributes true in the life, death, and resurrection of Christ.

Getting an explanation from God for your suffering will do little to comfort or satisfy you if you do not have confidence in the holiness and goodness of God. If you live under the notion that God is against you, then you could have all the answers but you would still have a troubled heart. However, if you know that God has perfect integrity and perfect love, then you can live in peace with no answers at all. God's character enables doubt and tranquility to coexist.

Doubt in Your Worst Nightmare

If you believe that you have to put on the appearance of strength and suppress all your questions, then you are wrong. You totally misunderstand what God desires from you. God wants a real relationship, and he wants your personal trust. He wants you to pour out your heart to him. Certainly, we always come before the living God with humility and reverence. At the same time, King David was utterly raw in his lamentations in the Psalms. God is a big boy (understatement of the century); he can handle it.

Do not shame yourself for your confusion. You are a fallen human being with very limited understanding. Of course you don't comprehend everything! God knows this too. He created you . . . and all of creation. He knows your capabilities. God is not surprised that you are frustrated and confused during your season of excruciating pain.

As you go to God with your doubts, I encourage you to maintain reasonable expectations on understanding why your personal tragedy has occurred. You probably will never receive a satisfactory explanation in the here and now for why this all happened. In heaven you will get it, and you will be satisfied and even grateful. For now, you will have to live in mystery.

Remember what Scripture and Christ have revealed to us about the goodness and trustworthiness of God. Understandably, our painful experiences may cause us to question this reality. The reassurance of God's character will give you greater peace and comfort than any explanation for why this all happened. Focus on God's character.

The Narrative of Hope

When I am confused and frustrated, I can express these feelings to God. I can share my doubts with him. I am a human being and not capable of fully comprehending why my child died. God knows this; he loves and accepts me anyway. I can be honest with God. Never will I have a satisfactory explanation in this life, but I take comfort in knowing that God is good and his ways are perfect.

Fear not, for I have redeemed you;
I have called you by name, you are mine.
When you pass through the waters, I will be with you;
and through the rivers, they shall not overwhelm you.

Isaiah 43:1–2

8

Presence

The emotional pains of your Worst take on a variety of forms. People experience disappointment, fear, anxiety, guilt, shame, anger, misunderstanding, and despair among other unpleasant feelings. One emotional aspect of suffering, however, tends to stand out as the most surprising and perhaps the hardest.

Jesus clearly understood this core component of suffering because he addressed it repeatedly in the Farewell Discourses of the Gospel of John. In John 14–17, Jesus prepared his disciples for the intense trials ahead. In spite of Christ's warnings about his forthcoming death, the disciples appeared to stand somewhere between naïve and unaware of the impending difficulties.

In this section of John leading up to his death, Jesus repeatedly exhorted his friends not to let their "hearts be troubled" (John 14:1, 27). He gave hints that the world would revile them, that religious leaders would throw them out of synagogues, and that their opponents would even kill them. Jesus warned them of their own spiritual failures, telling them that they would scatter and abandon him (see John 16:32).

In response to these predictions, Jesus's promises speak to this central ailment of suffering—*isolation*. You do not expect it, and you do not see it coming, but suffering can be so, so lonely.

When your Worst first strikes, people huddle around you. People constantly come in and out of your home. You're invited to dinner or to social gatherings. After a few months or weeks, the rush of people dissipates. People return to their normal lives. They do not ask as often about how you are doing.

Whether it is real or not, you start to feel left behind. You wake up in sorrow each day and feel as if people no longer notice or have forgotten. As the distance of time increases between the present day and your Worst, you feel more and more alone.

This is particularly true many years after your Worst. Your tragedy represents such an integral part of your story. You feel as if a person cannot understand you unless they know that you lost a child, a parent, a spouse, or that you experienced some sort of trauma in your life. An undercurrent of grief still persists in your consciousness at some level most of the time. You meet people who do not know about your past, and this wordless voice inside says, "This person is never going to understand me unless they know . . ."

That people don't know the perpetual sorrow that exists or that they don't know this pivotal chapter of your story creates a sense of alienation that you never expected.

This loneliness constitutes one of the most bitter and painful elements of your suffering.

Jesus understood the challenge of isolation that his friends would encounter after his death. Imagine the sense of alienation they felt after Christ died and many had forsaken him. Imagine carrying out the cause of Christ without their leader physically present. Imagine how misunderstood they felt as they tried to lead others into the new covenant and were met with resistance and violence.

Therefore, the promises of the Farewell Discourses largely revolve around the companionship of God. He comforted the disciples by saying that he would not "leave [them] as orphans" (John 14:18). Their story would not be one of abandonment.

Jesus first promised his resurrection. He told them that he would come to them after he died. His death would not be final.

Christ then foretold the coming of the Holy Spirit, whom he called the Helper or Comforter. Jesus assured the disciples that the Spirit would "convict," "guide," and "speak" to them (John 16:8, 13). The very person of God would continually live with and lead his people.

Out of these aforementioned promises came, perhaps, the most soothing assurance—union with Christ. Jesus pledged to abide in the hearts of the disciples as they abided in him. In other words, Jesus said that he would permanently reside in their hearts while they, in a mysterious but real way, dwelled in him.

All these promises assured the disciples of the permanent presence of God. These promises anticipated the loneliness that accompanies any suffering person.

Why is it that Jesus himself repeatedly concentrated his preparation for suffering on God's presence? Why does Jesus harp on this theme to his disciples?

Because Jesus knew the isolation of suffering better than anyone.

As a child, Jesus and his family became refugees when Herod sought to kill him. They were uprooted from their community.

Then, in his ministry, the Jewish leaders rejected Jesus and shut him out from their fellowship. As he led his movement, Christ had "no place to lay his head."

Jesus also knew the loneliness of being misunderstood. His own people, the Jews, largely considered him a heretic and blasphemer. Until the cross, his disciples never really "got" Jesus. When Elijah and Moses appeared at the Transfiguration, the disciples treated Jesus as if he were either equal or inferior to these Old Testament icons. When he told his disciples that he must die for the sins of the world, Peter rebuked Christ. Even his closest friends did not understand his mission and the sorrowful tasks that lay ahead of him on the cross.

Still, the alienation of these aspects of his life did not compare to the isolation that came as he approached his death.

At the peak of his anguish, when he asked his friends to stay up with him while he prayed, his friends repeatedly fell back asleep. Christ was all alone.

As the Romans arrested Jesus, his friends denied and disowned him. Christ was all alone.

When he took on the sins of the world, he was separated from the Father. Christ was all alone.

Christ reinforced his steadfast companionship with his disciples because he knew what awaited them—both looking ahead to and looking back on his own Worst. Jesus spoke from the firsthand experience of isolation. He taught from the trenches.

These promises that Christ made to his disciples extend to us as well. As Christ offered these comforts, visualize him exhorting you. See Jesus saying, "I will never leave you." When it feels as if the crowd has left, hear him insisting, "I am here, standing with you." When you feel as if you are walking alone, listen to him reminding you, "I always dwell in your heart. You carry me everywhere." When you long for his physical presence, hear him promise, "One day, I will come for you in the flesh."

Perhaps the sweetest word Christ calls to us is "You are not alone."

Being Abandoned

A common challenge that many people who have suffered tragedies face is being abandoned by friends. Many have commented that abandonment constitutes one of the most surprising and hurtful aspects of the grief process.

Nancy and David Guthrie are experts on grief and child loss. This couple has lost two children: their daughter, Hope, and son, Gabe. Through hosting retreats and writing books, they have used their tragedies to minister to others who have lost children.

In retreats and books, the Guthries dedicate significant attention to healing from and forgiving those who disappointed or avoided child-loss sufferers during their darkest hours. The stories I have heard in this vein have stunned me.

A mother who lost her child to cancer once told me about seeing a friend in a store who immediately turned and walked away when they chanced to see each other from a distance. Another couple said they had close friends they never heard from again after their son died suddenly.

Child-loss victims are not alone in this type of disappointment. An acquaintance of mine in New York had close friends who still have not contacted her over ten years after her cancer diagnosis.

People who have shared stories generally assume that for many of their absent friends, the intensity of the grief and darkness was too overwhelming for them to enter into. The tragedy struck too close to their friends' deepest fears, and they simply avoided it. For some people, they become paralyzed with the anxiety of not knowing what to say or do, and they end up never entering the situation at all.

I had very few people—close to nobody—disappoint or abandon me. In one situation, though, a friend popped his head in briefly when Cam died, and then he avoided the situation from then on. I did struggle with resentment toward this person.

I would find myself stewing a bit from time to time over this friend's relational distance, even two years after Cam had passed away. I would be on a jog or in the car, and this man would come to mind, and I held him with contempt.

One day I determined that I needed to wrestle with the Lord and examine my sin of resentment toward this person until God gave me relief. After an hour of journaling and praying and talking out loud to God, I finally identified what made me so angry about this person avoiding my tragedy: he had options.

He had options, and I did not.

He could choose to enter into my pain or to avoid it. I had no choice. I had to wake up every day with a break in my heart. I had to pass by Cam's empty bed. I had to see my dead child's pictures on the wall, cry over Cam's absence on birthdays and holidays, and dread the anniversary of his death. I could not escape my pain. I was locked in for life.

My friend had an option. He put his toe in the water, the water was uncomfortable, and he chose to leave.

This realization immediately moved me toward greater appreciation for Christ.

Why?

Because Jesus Had Options

The incarnation stands at the center of the Christian story. Jesus had dwelled in paradise for eternity. He never had experienced firsthand the painful state of the fallen world, nor did he have to. The mess of the broken earth was none of his doing. However, Christ regarded the beleaguered state of mankind with compassion.

Jesus had options. Christ could have opted out, but he entered in.

John describes Christ's coming in this ever-so-personal manner: "The Word became flesh and dwelt among us" (John 1:14). In modern times, we might translate this: "God decided to become a human being so that he could live with us." The incarnation demonstrates God's affinity toward brokenness.

The psalmist writes, "The Lord is near to the brokenhearted" (Ps. 34:18). This statement tells us so much about the personality and character of God.

Luke clearly depicted Jesus's attraction to sufferers in the story where Christ heals both the dying daughter of Jairus and the woman who continually discharged blood. In the story, a crowd of "fans" surrounded Jesus. Word of his power and teaching had spread. Jesus received "rock star" attention.

However, in the midst of this acclamation, his concern resided with those in suffering. Jairus, a leader of the local synagogue, bowed before Jesus and begged him to come to his house where his daughter was dying. As Jesus started to travel to the home, a woman who had continually discharged blood for a dozen years and had spent all her money seeking a medical solution touched Jesus from behind. This touch expressed a desperate need for healing.

Jesus had competing urgencies upon him. A crowd of fans pressed against him. Jesus was rushing to a home to heal a dying child. In the midst of the commotion and emergency, Jesus paused.

He stopped.

What could distract his attention from such priorities?

Christ asked, "Who was it that touched me?" (Luke 8:45). It sounds like a bizarre question in the given situation.

Out from the crowd emerged the ill woman. She trembled and fell down before Jesus. She explained her condition and revealed that Jesus had healed her.

Why does Jesus take (or, in the eyes, of a modern audience, *waste*) the time to ask this question? After all, the woman had received the physical healing she needed. The job was done.

Christ knew the deep alienation of this woman. He knew that her chronic discharge had prohibited her from entering the temple to worship for over a decade. He knew that her condition prevented her from being touched by others, because it would make them unclean to worship in the temple. He knew the woman needed healing from her deep isolation as much as she needed physical healing.

Jesus called her out so that the woman would know that God saw her pain. He called her out so that she could be face-to-face with the living God. He called her out so that she would know that God was *with her*. He called her out in order to heal the loneliness of her suffering.

Jesus's word for the woman was *daughter*. Jesus replied, "Daughter, your faith has made you well; go in peace" (Luke 8:48). Jesus saw the alienation of this woman as tantamount to the failing health of Jairus's dying daughter.

There was a crowd to please, a movement to grow, a message to proclaim, a kingdom to build—and where was Jesus?

Jesus's heart remained with the suffering and sick, the lonely and brokenhearted.

Jesus's heart still remains with the suffering and sick, the lonely and brokenhearted. His heart remains with you in the loneliness of your Worst.

In the midst of the global crises of poverty, injustice, war, and epidemic, God's heart still remains with the brokenhearted. He still draws near to you and enters into your pain in your Worst.

Jesus becomes the friend who sees all of your pain and suffering. He sticks his toe in the water, and it's boiling—it's utterly seething. In response, Jesus dives into the waters of your pain. He immerses himself in your pain.

God's Actual Presence versus His Perceived Presence

These assurances of God's companionship in the midst of your Worst may help, but what happens when you in no way *feel* the presence of God?

Two months after Cam died, an ice storm left people stranded for several days in their cars, offices, and homes throughout Birmingham. I made it out to the home of my friends, Oscar and Emily.

That night a neighbor's rap at the side door ignited boyishness throughout the home. The neighbor knew that Oscar had a three-year-old son, Ford, one of Cam's best friends. He offered his classic Flexible Flyer sled for my friend and his son to enjoy in the snow the next day.

The inner eight-year-old in me erupted. I may have been thirty-four, but I went to bed that night dreaming of sledding the steep hills in this mountainous neighborhood.

The next day, Oscar, Ford, and I embarked on our sledding adventure. I blazed the first tracks, flying six inches above the snow. Feeling the blistering, cold wind chap my face was no less exhilarating than when I was ten years old. A huge grin filled my face all the way to the base of the hill, where Ford and Oscar awaited me.

With the run tested and approved, I walked up the hill with Oscar and Ford for their inaugural ride down the hill. What a moment for Ford! His first sled ride! The father-son pair boarded the sled, and I gave them a nice push to give them some momentum. The adrenaline and excitement of the winter fun blinded me from a reality until my hands released Oscar's winter jacket.

There before me was my friend and his son. Here was I, atop the hill, standing alone. There would be no father-son journey for me. With every foot of progress my friends made down the hill, the stinging realization of my child's absence intensified.

Cam was not standing beside me playing in the snow. He was not waiting at my hip for his turn to board the sled. He was not asking me a thousand questions about snow and snowmen and sleds and snowballs. He was not giggling at the sight of yellow urine in the white snow after a quick toddler potty break.

The sled traveled over a crest near the bottom of the hill and out of my sight. I could see no one. I stood by myself at the top of the hill with salty tears forming in my eyes, made bloodshot by the chilling winds.

I looked through the parting of pine trees into the gray-clouded sky. Theologically, I knew that God was with me. Experientially, it was one of the loneliest moments of my life.

In a sermon on Psalm 22, Tim Keller made the distinction between the "perceived" presence of God and the "actual" presence of God.[8] At times, we can cognitively know God's presence while not existentially feeling it.

Keller explains that the cross gives believers the assurance that God never truly abandons them. When Jesus cried "My God, my God, why have you forsaken me?" on the cross, God "actually" forsook Jesus as he took on the sin of mankind (Ps. 22:1; Matt. 27:46). God the Father was "actually" separated from his Son. Jesus was "actually" alone in every possible way.

Keller proclaims that God abandoned Jesus in order that he never would have to abandon his people. Jesus "actually" experienced this abandonment on our behalf.

In your Worst, you will feel hung out to dry. You will feel distance from God, but that comprises only an emotional or existential reality—not a spiritual or theological one.

When we feel as if God is a million miles away, in reality he draws near to us. That is not a truth that we always feel in our hearts, but it is one we must cling to in our heads.

Jesus's life, death, and resurrection have created a reality where absolutely nothing can separate us from the love of God (Rom. 8:35–39).

Presence in Your Worst Nightmare

The saddest day of your life may be the loneliest day of your life too. You are not unique in feeling totally isolated. You are not a sub-par person or an inadequate Christian if you feel as if God has distanced himself from you. Most sufferers share this experience.

While you may feel distant from God, you must know that the propensity of God is to draw close to the brokenhearted. God leans into your suffering. Furthermore, one of the fundamental promises of the gospel is that Jesus Christ permanently dwells in your heart when you ask him into your life. He never leaves you.

Understand that God has not left you, even if your experience suggests that he has. In reality, God wants to stand by you. He abandoned his own Son, Jesus, so that he would never have to forsake you.

Nothing can separate you from the love of God. You have a steadfast companion in every moment in the Lord God. He stands at your side. You remain in his arms. Always.

The Narrative of Hope

I am not alone. I may feel isolated, but the Lord never will turn his back on me. Nothing I can do will make him walk away. In my suffering, Jesus draws near to me. God always remains at my side, and I remain in his arms forever. Nothing can stand between the Lord and me.

For the wages of sin is death, but the free gift of God is eternal life in Christ Jesus our Lord.

Romans 6:23

9

Sin

When Cam died, I knew that an enemy lurked in my midst that could stand in the way of my healing. It was an enemy whom many in suffering naturally befriend.

Early in my grief process, I started surveying blogs about coping with the loss of a child. On one online publication, a blogger asked parents who had lost children to offer advice to other bereaved parents in the comments section of the blog. Here I saw that this enemy had taken two people captive.

One father advised that parents should listen to their instincts. The pediatrician had believed that the child's symptoms did not warrant hospitalization; they sounded like a common cold, based on the doctor's and the dad's phone consultation. Tragically, the daughter died from a rare disease. The father claimed that he annually called the doctor on his daughter's birthday to remind him of his error and to tell him how old she would have been on that day if the doctor had not failed. After the first few years, the doctor declined his call, but the father left a venomous reminder on the answering machine for sixteen consecutive years.

Another father bluntly said that he would tell parents, "If there is a God, then he plays favorites." This bitter jab of sarcasm was the entirety of his advice.

More than a decade after these two dads lost their children, excruciating pain still oozed from their comments. The enemy seemed to be winning the battle in both situations.

Nothing can destroy a hurting person more than bitterness, but how difficult it is to resist!

Five months after Cam died, I stood at a whiteboard, diagramming the basics of salvation for a group of sixth graders.

Phone rings. Wife. Screaming and weeping. Drop the pen. Sprinting out the door. Nearly hyperventilating. Speeding to the hospital. Heart racing. More doom.

Lauren was three months into our completely unplanned and unexpected pregnancy. Something had occurred that could only be interpreted as a miscarriage. Lauren called me weeping as she drove to the hospital.

Contrary to our expectation, the baby was still alive. However, the situation was tenuous, and we would have to go to the OB/GYN every week to check for a heartbeat.

There is no way to sugarcoat this: I was enraged. I was full of anger. And I directed my anger at God.

I had gone through enough. My kid had died. I was already reeling from that tragedy. Now I had a weekly appointment to ascertain whether or not I would have a second child perish within six months.

It felt cruel.

Wasn't there equity in suffering? Didn't pain get evenly distributed? Why had the onslaught of misery in my life not stopped?

After several weekly visits to the obstetrician, my anger swelled. I just could not shake the seeming unfairness of it all. I knew that anger would lead to resentment, and resentment to bitterness. I knew bitterness would poison my soul. However, nothing would quell my anger. I could not talk myself out of it.

Relief and protection finally came from an unexpected truth.

The Paradoxical Freedom of Acknowledging Our Sin

There are very few things a person can do to produce and prolong misery like ignoring one's own sin. Conversely (and surprisingly), there are very few things a person can do to elicit relief and freedom like confessing his or her sins to God.

The latter statement sounds so counterintuitive. Sin carries such negative connotations. It reminds us of our faults, shortcomings, and limitations. Who wants to examine, own, and admit the worst aspects of his or her thoughts and actions?

However, I have not found a more effective means for deliverance from the misery of bitterness than to remember my own sinfulness. And trust me, if you have not experienced the exhausting, heart-hardening, and thought-consuming darkness of bitterness, you eventually *will* want a way out when you encounter it.

Bitterness initially feels so good—you feel so justified and so in control. You feel "right." You are the victim. Bitterness can feel like a nice alternative to the pain you ordinarily feel in your Worst. However, it will corrode your soul and steal your joy over time. Bitterness on top of the pain of your Worst can make your inner life a living hell.

In Luke 16, Jesus told the story of a rich man who experienced *literal* hell. This rich man, who never repented from his transgressions or reconciled with God while on earth, lived permanently, eternally stuck in his sin. In this story, we can see a central aspect of sin that can plague those living in their Worst.

On earth the rich man lived a comfortable life, where he showed no humility before God and no compassion to his poor neighbor Lazarus. From Hades he saw Abraham in heaven and called for him to send Lazarus to give him a drink of water to ease the torment. When Abraham said that he could not grant such a request, the rich man then asked Abraham to send a messenger to his family to warn them of the anguish that could await them in the afterlife if they did not repent (Luke 16:19–31).

Even though the rich man was living under the judgment of God and had seen the futility of his earthly ways, he continued to regard Lazarus as if he were an inferior servant. The rich man continued to believe that he deserved to be served. He continued to demonstrate an unrelenting sense of entitlement, believing at the core that he deserved better.

Sin naturally deludes us into thinking that we are the center of the universe. It whispers in our ears: *You know, you really are pretty good. Sure you have made some mistakes, but compared to most, you're a good person. You're a little more important than everyone else. If blessings come your way, it's because you've earned them. Since you're generally good—at least better than most—God owes you.*

Conversely, when tragedy and disappointment pierce our lives, sin speaks another set of lies rooted in the same conceptual fallacy. Sin says: *You deserve better than this. After all you've done, this is the treatment you get from God? You're a good person. You're entitled to better. God has wronged you.*

Here resides a pathway to inner misery. I know this road well, and every brick along the way is filled with lies. With every step, resentment toward God increases as one moves closer and closer to the final destination: miserable bitterness.

One can contrast the reaction of the rich man in Luke 16 with the posture of King David when his opponent, Shimei, came out to curse him on the road. David had retreated from Jerusalem after his son Absalom had seized his throne. Shimei, who had sided with King Saul many years before, believed that David had unjustly risen to his kingship after Saul's demise. He called David "evil," "worthless," and a "man of blood" (2 Sam. 16:7–8). Shimei cursed David, wishing misfortune to fall upon him.

David's servant, who stood next to David as Shimei cursed him, responded with outrage, wanting to cut off Shimei's head, but David rebuked his servant. David suggested that perhaps God had commanded Shimei to curse him. Perhaps God intended to bring calamity on David. If so, David asked, then who was he to resist the will of God—regardless of its painfulness?

David exhibited an attitude full of humility and absent of entitlement. He believed he should be no more exempt from difficulty by the hand of God than anyone else.

An incredibly gracious woman I know demonstrated similar humility when doctors diagnosed her with cancer. Everyone said "Why you? Why you?" to this saint and pillar of the community. They believed that her kindness, philanthropy, and generosity should insulate her from life's difficulties.

Her response: "Why not me?" There was a meekness that communicated she felt no more worthy of comfort and no more exempt from pain than the next person.

What enabled David to accept his potential sufferings with such calm acceptance and meekness? David had lost his kingdom largely because of his own moral shortcomings. He was running from Absalom because of his own failures. The former king had essentially raped a married woman, Bathsheba. To cover up his violation, he arranged the murder of her husband, Uriah (2 Samuel 11). Due largely to the intervention of his friend, the prophet Nathan, David saw the severity of his sin.

In Psalm 51, a song where David laments his sin over this aforementioned scandal, he confessed to God,

> For I know my transgressions,
> and my sin is ever before me.
> Against you, you only, have I sinned
> and done what is evil in your sight,
> so that you may be justified in your words
> and blameless in your judgment. (vv. 3–5)

David knew his sins and declared that God is justified in any judgments he may administer in his life.

Acknowledging my sin, which mitigated my sense of entitlement, repeatedly protected me from bitterness. My anger was grounded in the belief that God owed me a better, more comfortable life. Deep in my heart, perhaps I believed that because I worked in ministry, or had always attended church, or had not forsaken God after Cam died, God should limit my suffering to some degree.

Our sin nature leads us to relate to God based on performance. Our sinfulness deceives us into thinking that we can earn God's favor. When God forgives our sins and brings us into relationship with him, we do not like to accept that our salvation comes entirely as a product of God's grace and mercy. We want to believe that at least some merit on our part—even if it's just a tiny shred—has obliged God to love us.

Clinging to that one little shred of supposed merit opens the door to potential madness. If we believe that the holy God owes us anything, then anger swells and distance grows when life does not go our way.

As crazy as it may sound, when I found myself becoming angry and entitled, I would write down the twenty worst things that I had ever done or thought in my life. I would ask the Holy Spirit to reveal my sin. Knowing that God completely accepted me through Christ enabled me to lay all my dark deeds on the table.

By the end of this catalogue of my sins, I felt closer to the Lord and increasingly freed from my anger. I had to accept the bitter pill: Because of my sin, I had earned only judgment from a perfect, holy God who had created me. However, God had given me forgiveness, righteousness, adoption, heaven, and his eternal presence *out of his generosity*, not out of obligation.

Not a Contract-Based Relationship

Now, I realize this chapter runs the risk of being misunderstood. One could read what I have written so far and think, *Is this jerk saying that I'm getting what I deserve? Is he saying that I'm utterly corrupt and evil; therefore God is punishing me?*

Absolutely not.

What I am saying is that the gospel changes the dynamics of our relationship with God.

We naturally think that what God brings into our lives is a reaction to our deeds. We reason that our circumstances are a reflection of the way God feels about us. Therefore, we are prone to think, *Haven't I earned better than this?* or *Why does God hate me?* when we experience tragedy.

The cross disrupts and ends this cause-and-effect mode of thinking.

The gospel means that we do not live in a contract-based relationship with the Lord. Christ's cross ends a karma orientation in our relationship with him. When we encounter our Worst, it does not mean that God has failed on his end of the bargain. He never owed us anything in the first place.

Simultaneously, when tragedy enters our lives, it does not necessarily mean that God is punishing us for some failure or disobedience. God no longer punishes us; he punished Jesus on the cross for our sins to free us from his wrath. After we become believers by reconciling with God through Christ, God relates to us, his adopted children, based on the merits and obedience of Jesus Christ—not based on our failures.

God does use our sufferings to teach us and to shape our character. However, he does not strike us down as one seeking retribution and vengeance. On the cross, Jesus absorbed all of God's vengeance that the Lord might possibly direct toward us.

God did this because he loves us. Yes, we are sinners. Yes, we have earned the disfavor of God in our sins. But God considers our lives so valuable and precious that "while we were still sinners, Christ died for us" (Rom. 5:8).

Remembering our sins and then remembering the grace of God through Christ removes us from the contract-based orientation to God that can generate such entitlement and bitterness. It prevents us from thinking that our relationship with God is *quid pro quo*. It stops our tendency to hold God to our flawed, human standards of fairness.

Our arguments of entitlement die at the cross. In this way, the cross protects us from the danger of bitterness. The cross provides a startling juxtaposition: we see that Jesus lived a perfect, sinless life, and yet all he received on earth was pain and suffering. Christ never sinned, and yet he was betrayed, misunderstood, mocked, beaten, and tortured. He did nothing to receive the wrath of God, and yet his life ended on the cross, bearing the sins of man and experiencing separation from the Father.

When we feel as if God has treated us unfairly, it helps to remember the treatment of Jesus on earth. When we feel as if we deserve better, the cross can stop that thought in its tracks, because we certainly do not believe that we are entitled to a more comfortable life than Jesus. This line of thinking protects us from bitterness and restores us to peace with the Lord.

Sin in Your Worst Nightmare

Bitterness and anger stand as the biggest threats to your healing and recovery during the day of your worst nightmare. Anger can feel so good and justified at times, but it will corrode your soul and your life.

Accepting the reality and consequence of your sin protects you from this mortal enemy. As painful as this may be to hear, God does not owe us anything. Knowing this truth will undermine any sense of entitlement that underlies resentment toward God.

Your suffering is not a form of divine punishment. Jesus removed God's wrath toward you on the cross. In spite of your sin, God loves you. The cross shows the full extent of God's love for you too.

Life, according to human terms, is not fair. No person knows this better than Jesus himself. When you start to feel resentment toward the Lord, remember the unfairness that Jesus experienced even though he lived as a sinless person. It reminds you and me that nobody deserves a better, more comfortable life than Jesus.

The Narrative of Hope

Bitterness is my biggest enemy in the season of my Worst. I am a sinner to whom God owes nothing. I am not entitled to anything and cannot resent God. God is not punishing me. Jesus removed whatever judgment I earned through my sins. In spite of my sin, God loves me through Christ.

Section 3

THE LONG HAUL

I will turn their mourning into joy;
I will comfort them, and give them gladness for sorrow.

Jeremiah 31:13

10

Joy

One of the most discouraging comments people said to me after my tragic loss was "You'll see him again one day," or "This will all be made right in heaven." Despite the good intentions and theological accuracy of such statements, what I heard was, "The next time you'll be happy again is when you die," as if I was sentenced to permanent sadness.

One of the most depressing fears that people face in the wake of their Worst is the feeling that they never will be happy again. Hobbies that once added so much excitement to life seem worthless. Who now cares about mountain biking, shopping, or watching sports? The vigor and passion of your vocation feels meaningless. That drive that got you out of bed in the morning evaporates. The annual vacation that you looked forward to all year now may be a point of dread.

Happiness seems impossible. Happiness seems out of reach.

Psychologists use the term *anhedonia* to describe losing the sense of pleasure that one previously experienced before a loss.

Moments or activities that previously elicited great excitement no longer have such an effect. Anhedonia is common for those in grief.

I often found myself thinking, *Life is over*. I thought that I would just need to learn to deal with trudging through the rest of my life and learning to accept permanent discontentment.

In Psalm 40, after describing God's redemption in his life, the psalmist speaks of the Lord putting a "new song" in his mouth (Ps. 40:3). The rock band U2 expressed this sentiment in the song "40," based on this psalm, by singing, "Now I sing, sing a new song."[9]

I needed a new song of my own, and the Lord delivered it through one providential email.

On the day after Cam died, I opened my email to over five hundred new messages. As I scanned my bloated inbox, my eye landed on the urgent subject line of one email: "Get this to Cameron."

More than the subject, though, the credibility of the sender gave my heart comfort in that desperate time. The sender was an old family friend, Henry, who had lost a child seventeen years before. I immediately identified with him and remembered the way that Henry and his wife, Judy, still deeply loved Jesus and how their lives continued to thrive after their daughter, Dine, passed away.

In the email, Henry shared the story of how nearly losing his second son to serious illness prepared him for the nightmarish reality of suddenly losing their daughter a decade later. Henry's email became instrumental in God giving me hope for the future. Henry informed me that their second son, Vaughn, had been born with a life-threatening pulmonary condition. Early on, Henry had to confront the possibility that one day he could experience the death of a child. Vaughn miraculously survived, but this frightening season provided a foundation for when their worst nightmare, indeed, came true over a decade later in the death of their daughter.

Henry closed his email with these pivotal words:

> When Dine died in Chicago seventeen Septembers ago, God called His Word and His promise back to me. She no longer could come to me, but surely (as I live, breathe, and worship) I will go to her. This comfort led us through the years of grief that Judy and I faced at that time with the active promise from our Father that if we would lean into the grief He would surely bring us to. He would get us through it to a point where the death of precious Dine would no longer sting, and that her memory in every way would bring us joy. And so, according to the promise, has it been. This is our prayer for you all and I believe the earnestness of the promise God has for you. God Bless You . . .

Henry articulated a radical concept of Christianity: the promise that God can turn all sorrow and sadness into joy. He promised that God could transform our Worst such that, in time, Cam's memory would no longer devastate us but could bring us deep joy.

Joy became the new song.

Understanding the difference between happiness and joy is an important delineation during your Worst. Happiness is a blessing that comes from the Lord, but happiness is circumstantially dependent. Everything in your life must line up right and go your way in order to experience happiness. When your circumstances are painful, difficult, or disappointing, happiness disappears. I felt very little happiness in the year after Cam's death.

Happiness also possesses a fleeting nature. You feel happy the night of a concert, after a big success, or at a great party, but happiness dissipates quickly.

Furthermore, happiness is shallow. It affects your emotions but does not penetrate deep into your spirit.

Not so with joy—joy possesses a deep and steadfast quality that far surpasses happiness.

In my Worst, I found that joy came from two primary places: (1) intimacy with God, and (2) seeing Christ's redemption and healing in my life.

I found intimacy with God by seeking closeness in relationship with him. I sought to know him more deeply through prayer, praise, fellowship, and Bible reading. I wanted and needed to experience his presence.

In Psalm 16, the psalmist declares,

> You make known to me the path of life;
>   in your presence there is fullness of joy;
>   at your right hand are pleasures forevermore. (Ps. 16:11)

He links intimacy with God with the richest joy. The psalmist describes how God leads him to his divine presence, the place of deep, spiritual gladness.

Psalm 21 expresses a similar sentiment. In this psalm, a king rejoices at the blessings he has received from God, but his joy does not come from this good fortune. He sings, "For you make him most blessed forever; you make him glad with the joy of your presence" (Ps. 21:6). In spite of all the great blessings that a king can receive, he derives his deepest joy in knowing the glorious presence of the Lord.

Because you can find joy in closeness with God, this means that you can experience it, regardless of your circumstances.

James tells his audience "Count it all joy, my brothers, when you meet trials of various kinds" (James 1:2). He points to the possibility for joy and suffering to coexist. In fact, James may even suggest that joy can increase when trials arise because you must trust and draw near to the Lord even more.

In Paul's letter to the Philippians, gladness, optimism, and joy fill his voice. However, Paul scribed this letter from prison, while uncertainty surrounded his survival.

Paul mentioned rejoicing seven different times in this short book. He came to see and know who God is through Christ. His personal knowledge of and fellowship with the Lord produced a joy that enlivened and sustained Paul in his suffering.

Because deep joy flows out of intimacy with God, it constitutes one of the greatest comforts in your Worst. Your circumstances are terrible and will be for some time. Happiness, for the most part, is off the table. Nothing, though, can separate you from the love of God. Nothing, apart for your own sin, can distance you from him. Therefore, pursuing intimacy with Christ through prayer, Scripture, worship, and fellowship comprises one of the most important and hopeful steps in your Worst. I recommend seeking to maximize your joy by seeking intimacy with Christ as one of the wisest moves you can make.

Henry's email strummed the first chords of a new song in my Worst. God gave me a foundation for hope. I was not sentenced to misery forever. When people asked me how they could pray for me, I always asked them to pray that I would have intimacy with God and deep joy in the days and weeks after Cam died. God graciously granted me one of the most connected seasons with him that I have ever encountered. I don't miss the sadness and pain of the year following Cam's death, but I do miss the rich joy that I experienced in my relationship with Christ.

Because of the misery that greeted me each morning, I had no alternative but to seek deeper fellowship with Christ. No hobby, success, or possession offered any potential for joyfulness on a given day. My idols, which seemed so promising in the ordinary seasons of life, all fell flat. I could see their impotence and futility so clearly. Jesus consistuted the only positive option for joy in my heart. Out of desperation, I sought him in a way unlike any other time in my life.

Isn't that a counterintuitive thought? You can have more joy in the season of your Worst than in any previous time in life. In your Worst, you become dependent on God like no time before. Out of this dependency comes intimacy with Jesus that can yield such joy. This reality demonstrates the radical power of knowing Christ through the gospel.

Experiencing Joy by Seeing Christ

Not only did I find joy through closeness with Christ, but I also experienced joy when I saw God's redemptive work during my Worst. Pastor John Piper has defined joy as "a good feeling in the soul, produced by the Holy Spirit, as he causes us to see the beauty of Christ in the Word and in the world." *Perhaps there is no better way to see the beauty and goodness of Jesus than by witnessing him heal your heart and restore your life.*

One must search exhaustively to find a more traumatic suffering in the Bible than the one the Israelites faced in the Babylonian invasion and captivity. For many years, God's prophets had warned the Israelites that their enemies would conquer them if they continued to depend on false gods and rely on foreign allies rather than trusting the Lord. After decades of admonition, their worst-case scenario occurred.

The Babylonians, the fearsome superpower of the ancient Near East, devastated everything precious to God's people over the course of approximately a decade. They besieged the city of Jerusalem, starving out the citizens. Jeremiah described the hunger of the people as so dire that "compassionate mothers" cooked their own children for food (Lam. 4:10).

Then, the enemy burst through the supposedly impenetrable walls and gates of Jerusalem (Lam. 2:8–9). The former safe haven became a scene of massacre and atrocity.

They destroyed the sacred temple of God. The attackers ravaged the priceless gold and silver instruments for worship as if they were cheap prizes. The safe, holy place, which possessed the deep presence of God, now had pagan conquerors traipsing through it, profaning its sanctity. The high priest, who formerly interceded on behalf of the Jews and led them in worship, was marched to Babylon, where he was killed. In the end, the Babylonians destroyed the temple, leaving the crown jewel of Jerusalem in shambles.

Over decades, the invaders marched the survivors of the attack approximately 900 miles in desert-like conditions (Ezra 7:9). Worst of all, they uprooted the people from their treasured Promised Land back to a foreign country, where they lived as second-class citizens.

Few people ever will experience a trauma as deep as the exiled Jews. Anyone who survived the fall of Jerusalem witnessed atrocity and experienced anguish. They likely lost friends and relatives through violence or starvation, encountered life-threatening hunger and dehydration, and witnessed enemies ransack and demolish their precious homeland.

The prophet Jeremiah preached to the Jews just before and during the invasion. In Jeremiah 31, he foretold God's restoration of his people even before the captivity occurred. Here, he describes the survivors as those who "survived the sword" and "found grace in the wilderness" (Jer. 31:2). The ones who remained were those who avoided violent death in Jerusalem and fatal starvation during the desert journey.

This was not a "my iPhone keeps on running out of power" type of suffering; it was tragedy. I emphasize the nature of this tragedy because we often believe that God can offer joy to people with "first-world problems." However, we do not necessarily think that God's power to heal and offer joy can extend to victims of horrible tragedies or unthinkable loss. God can redeem a dating break-up, for example, but not a divorce. He can handle the death of a grandparent but not of a child or spouse. The Jews experienced virtual horror, and yet God made bold promises of future joy to them.

In addition, we tend to think that God's promises of joy apply to those who suffer as victims, but they do not apply to sinners. The audience of exiles contained two groups: the idolatrous perpetrators and the faithful remnant. God's promises of redemption and joy apply indiscriminately to both victims of injustice as well as those who have authored their own problems.

Even though Israel encountered catastrophe and, as a whole, caused their own downfall, God still sang a new song to the exiles.

The Lord pledged to restore the people and to fill them with gladness and joy. He proclaimed that "they shall come and sing aloud on the height of Zion, and they shall be radiant over the goodness of the Lord" (Jer. 31:12). God vowed to bring gladness to his people by showing them his glorious beauty as he brought them back from exile. He promised to show them his goodness through a redemptive work that touched all facets of their lives.

Jeremiah referred to future days of gladness following the exile. He talked about a time when the people would "adorn [themselves] with tambourines" and "go forth in the dance of the merrymakers," referring to a time when they would laugh, dance, and celebrate again (Jer. 31:4). The idea of enjoying a party or having a carefree celebration seems so foreign and infeasible to people in their Worst. God proclaims its possibility. He foreshadowed a day of emotional healing for the Jews, and he offers one to you as well.

The prophet announced that the Jews would once again "plant vineyards on the mountains of Samaria; the planters plant and shall enjoy the fruit" (Jer. 31:5). The ordinary joys of their vocation would return. In the early days of your Worst, the idea that you can find pleasure and motivation in your vocation feels impossible. Nevertheless, God promises the possibility of a functional life for those who feel crushed.

Finally, Jeremiah vowed that the day would come when the people would declare, "Let us go up to Zion to the Lord our God" (Jer. 31:6). He promised a return to the place of God's presence, the hill where the temple resided. God pledged that the people would worship the Lord with gladness. He would revive them from spiritual deadness and isolation. Many people in their saddest hours cannot fathom returning to church and singing hymns with gladness again, but God puts this possibility on the table.

Jeremiah pledged—even before the invasion actually occurred—a comprehensive redemption to these suffering people. He proclaimed that they would witness the Lord's healing activity in their lives. The fruit of seeing him work would be vibrant joyfulness in their hearts:

Their life shall be like a watered garden,
    and they shall languish no more.
Then shall the young women rejoice in the dance,
    and the young men and the old shall be merry.
I will turn their mourning into joy;
    I will comfort them, and give them gladness for sorrow.
        (Jer. 31:12–13)

The Lord can bring joy into our lives, even in our darkest hours. As we prayerfully trust God to redeem us, we gain the opportunity to see his work and to experience his joy, which comes from witnessing his healing hand in action. The more I prayed and trusted Christ with the challenges of my grief, the stronger and louder the new song of joy played in my heart.

This transition from mourning into joy does not occur in an instant. In Jeremiah 31, God pledged to bring the Israelites back to their land "by brooks of water" and via a "straight path" that he would prepare for them (v. 9). Their journey from exile back to the Promised Land was a long one through a desert. God is ready and able to lead sufferers in their arduous, uncomfortable journey through the desert back to a "promised land" of joy. While we can experience joy through intimacy with God at any moment, it takes time, patience, and the eyes of faith to find joy through witnessing his redemptive work.

If God can make a promise of future restoration and joy to such a traumatized group, then his redemption is possible for any person, regardless of how deep their suffering may be.

God Turns Sorrow into Joy

The sweetest and most hopeful promise that God makes to sufferers in relation to joy is his propensity to turn sorrow into joy.

God can take the very moments and memories of our Worst and turn them into objects that produce joy in our souls.

When I learned the necessity of seeking joy in my Worst, I recalled one of Christ's final words to his disciples. Knowing that he would die on the cross and realizing that the disciples were generally not ready for the tragedy, Jesus prepared them with a hopeful promise:

> Truly, truly, I say to you, you will weep and lament, but the world will rejoice. You will be sorrowful, but your sorrow will turn into joy. When a woman is giving birth, she has sorrow because her hour has come, but when she has delivered the baby, she no longer remembers the anguish, for joy that a human being has been born into the world. So also you have sorrow now, but I will see you again, and your hearts will rejoice, and no one will take your joy from you. (John 16:20–22)

Jesus candidly told the disciples that they would grieve and mourn. In the week of Jesus's arrest, sentencing, and death, can you imagine the inner crisis the disciples faced? They believed that Jesus was the Messiah of God who would deliver Israel from the Romans. They believed that they would inherit high positions in his political cabinet.

Now the Romans had executed their hero, rather than being defeated by him. The disciples were effectively outlaws, evading the authorities, rather than being high-ranking officers in Christ's kingdom. They watched their leader suffer excruciating pain on a cross, rather than reigning gloriously as they expected.

But Jesus sung the new song to them just as he did to me through Henry's pivotal email: God turns sorrow into joy. He turns weeping into dancing. He turns laments into celebration.

The disciples would look back at the apparent defeat and failure of Jesus's mission—they would look back on the cross—and see the most profound joy of their lives. God would take that symbol of agony and transform it into the greatest sign of joy-inducing love. The cross would become the greatest emblem of the joy of their salvation.

The Lord gave me a boldness in asking him to turn the debris of our tragedy into symbols of deep spiritual gladness.

About a week after Cam's death, I sat in our rocking chair and looked around his room, observing all of the remnants of Cam's life. I saw his sadly empty bed with the bedposts on each corner. I looked at the dresser that contained his adorable clothes. I admired his newborn portraits, taken at the hospital, hanging on the wall over his bed. I noticed the hundreds of books stacked on the shelf. I looked at a pile of laminated crafts that Cam made at Mother's Day Out events. These otherwise pleasant sights now represented the shattered glass of our lives.

As I looked at the remnants of a lost life and my shattered soul, nothing pained my ailing heart like Cam's green, Mickey Mouse underpants. Though it may sound peculiar, the underpants captured so much of my grief. They reminded me of our "rite of passage" trip to Target to purchase "big boy" underpants. They represented the pride I had in my all-star potty trainer, who conquered this mighty developmental milestone in about a week. He was growing up.

At the same time, these were the panties of a little boy. Here they lay unused on the floor, never to be worn again by their rightful owner.

The scene was wrong. The underpants screamed that little boys are not meant to die. Little boy underpants are not meant to be retired early.

As I lamented the sight, the Lord called Christ and Henry's new song back to me: *God turns sorrow into joy*. My mind had ruminated on this promise that God could redeem every detail of this tragedy. In what was a "stake in the ground" moment, I pointed my index finger at the underpants and said with full conviction, "Lord, redeem those underpants." I know this may sound silly—I mean, we are talking about undergarments after all—but this profound, determined hope flowed through my heart.

God can do it. God can redeem every—single—thing. God can even make underpants a symbol and source of joy. Why not ask and believe?

Three days later, Lauren and I traveled to Greenville to get out of Birmingham. As our daughter, Mary Matthews, dozed off to sleep, I noticed tears streaming down Lauren's face as she attempted to muffle her sobs. After unsuccessfully searching for a Kleenex, I saw out of the corner of my eye that Lauren had pulled a green and white garment from her purse to wipe away the tears. My heart leapt when I realized that Lauren was wiping away her tears with Cam's green, Mickey Mouse underpants. God showed me his faithfulness and his power. If he could redeem a pair of underpants, then certainly he could turn every last detail of our suffering into joy.

This incident was one of many ways I have seen God turn sorrow into joy. When I look back at Cam's funeral, it stands as one of the most joyful experiences of my life. I saw the support of God as hundreds of friends showed up. I experienced the presence of God in as profound a way as I ever can recall. I saw the reality and beauty of the gospel as never before, knowing that Christ's death and resurrection ensured that I would see my son again.

If God can make the remembrance of a child's funeral a most joyous and sweet memory, then he can redeem anything.

Joy in Your Worst Nightmare

Your life is not over. You are not finished. You may not emerge from this cloud of darkness for many years. The break in your heart may never fully heal; tears may remain with you for the rest of your life.

However, God can turn your sorrow into joy. He can turn your mourning into dancing. He can bring you to a place where the memory of your season of suffering induces joy.

Remember that joy and happiness are different. Happiness depends on good circumstances. Joy comes from intimacy with and trust in Christ. The possibility of joy transcends your situation.

No matter how deep your trauma, God can redeem your life and bring you to a state of joyfulness. No matter where your Worst takes you, God's power can bring joy to any person in any circumstance. Nothing is beyond the reach of Christ's redemptive arm.

You must know, though, that being brought to this place of joy requires two things: patience and faith. As my old pastor told me, "The love of God is slow." Do not be dismayed if you feel no joy in your life at this point. It will take some time.

Finally, you cannot generate joy on your own. Joy comes as a grace from God. It comes out of deep, abiding relationship with Jesus. Your role in the process involves asking him for joy. It involves trusting, abiding, and waiting on him.

I pray that God will surprise you in the same way that he has surprised me. I pray that you will hear God's voice singing you a new song.

The Narrative of Hope

My life is not over; my despair not permanent. I can have joy today—in this moment—through the presence of Christ. God can turn all my sorrow into joy, all my mourning into gladness, all my crying into dancing. Christ is making all things new. In his time, he can redeem the entirety of my pain and grief and give me a joyful life.

And I am sure of this, that he who began a good work in you will bring it to completion at the day of Jesus Christ.

Philippians 1:6

11

Service

A person can wish to die without being suicidal.

Anyone who has experienced tragedy knows this paradox. You are miserable. A dark cloud follows you at all times.

You have no real intentions or active plans of taking your life, but the idea of a truck running you over sounds pretty attractive. You do not want to check out, but you know with certainty that you are not happy on earth.

At the center of this malaise resides the struggle to find anything to live for. You repeatedly wrestle with the question, "Is life worth living?"

I once traveled to a nation in Asia on a mission trip to share the gospel with people, most of whom had never heard of Jesus in any form. I went to lunch with a college student named Stephen in the days after a devastating earthquake in his country. I told him that good things can come out of natural disasters and related the story of how I became a Christian during a tornado.

After hearing the gospel, Stephen asked an insightful question: "If, in Christ, you are bound for a perfect place in heaven, why remain on earth?"

It was a logical line of reasoning. Here was a young man who had read of how tens of thousands of his fellow countrymen had died in the earthquake. His family and friends lived with ever-present anxiety since they dwelled within an hour of the epicenter. People slept on lawns and in fields for fear that their homes might collapse in an aftershock. In the gospel, Stephen was introduced to heaven, a perfect place of no worries, death, or suffering. It made sense that an escape from the trials and anxieties of the world intrigued Stephen.

If one had a direct pathway to heaven through Christ, why not fast-track the journey there? If a person can escape from the trepidation and difficulty of the fallen world, why hang around this broken place?

In *Tracks of a Fellow Struggler*, author Reverend John Claypool, who lost his nine-year old daughter to leukemia, wrote: "Now that I am here, please stop the world; I want to get off!"[10]

About one month after Cam died, I more deeply comprehended the painful totality of our loss. I felt as if I had entered into a dark tunnel that never ended. Meanwhile, the only hopeful thing I could conjure up was the idea of being in heaven with Cam. Given that statistics projected that I probably had anywhere from forty to fifty more years left on this earth, I felt trapped and struggled for meaning.

I wallowed along one Saturday, languishing in a depressed stupor. The cold, cloudy day resembled my mood as I pitifully plodded around for hours in my pajamas and unkempt hair.

I continuously asked the question, "Is life worth living?" and could not find a positive answer. At the end of the day, I sat in bed defeated. I simply did not want to be alive.

Nevertheless, the Lord made something clear to me that night that helped me turn the corner. I had spent a day thinking continuously about how I did not want to be alive, but God, in an almost mystical manner, planted this thought in my head: "So you don't want to be alive, but do you really want to *die*?" God reminded me that he claims possession of my every breath and heartbeat. At any point, the Lord can call me home. As I lay there pondering the fragility of my life and the theoretical lack of guarantee I had for tomorrow, a sense of panic gripped me.

God impressed this truth upon me in a manner that scared me. In a sense, the Lord called my bluff.

When the possibility of actually dying appeared feasible, a fear immediately set in.

Do I really want to die?

NO!

I do not want to leave. I do not want to die. I want to be here. I want to be with my daughter and my wife. I want to share the gospel with people. I want to serve my students. I want to bear fruit for God's kingdom.

The motivations that instantly came to my mind exclusively related to eternal matters: serving God and loving people. There was something to live for. There were reasons to stick this life out, and they all pointed back to serving the Lord.

Paul, Confusion, and Service

These aforementioned yearnings to leave the world may strike someone as unfaithful or un-Christian. However, even the most faithful of Christians wrestles with the existential question of whether life is worth living after tragedy.

The apostle Paul expressed these sentiments multiple times. He had endured continuous trials and pain during his ministry.

Paul admitted in his second letter to the church at Corinth, "For we do not want you to be unaware, brothers, of the affliction we experienced in Asia. For we were so utterly burdened beyond our strength that we despaired of life itself" (2 Cor. 1:8). In modern terms, Paul effectively said, "We hated life."

Within this anguish Paul cited a yearning to leave the pain of this world and a desire to enter into the pleasure of eternal glory. He later said in 2 Corinthians, "While we are still in this tent, we groan, being burdened—not that we would be unclothed, but that we would be further clothed, so that what is mortal may be swallowed up by life" (2 Cor. 5:4). Again in Romans 8, Paul exclaims, "We ourselves, who have the firstfruits of the Spirit, groan inwardly as we wait eagerly for adoption as sons, the redemption of our bodies" (Rom. 8:23).

In both of these texts, he uses the raw, visceral language of "groaning." This term does not express slight desire but a longing that churns from the bowels of a person's soul.

The term "groaning" appears often in Scripture and also carries significance during the Israelites' time in Egypt. In Exodus, God's people "groaned" to be delivered from slavery (Ex. 2:23–24; 6:5). They suffered in their state of servitude and longed for the better place that God had promised Abraham and their forefathers. They deeply desired the relief of release from slavery and the pleasure of the land of "milk and honey" (Ex. 3:8).

Anyone who has ever experienced profound loss is totally familiar with such sentiments. When you begin to comprehend how drastically life has been altered, there appears to be no hope, no reason for going on, no possibility that there ever again could be anything worth living for.

A person can see and experience the brokenness of this world and imagine the perfect glory of heaven. This tension increases in the season of your Worst. The depth of the darkness of this world climaxes and your longing for relief—permanent relief—heightens.

For Paul, his tension was twofold. He loved Jesus and wanted to see him face-to-face. He craved the perfect joy and bliss of heaven.

At the same time, Paul also wanted relief from his suffering. He had undergone so much abuse, including unjust imprisonments, brutal beatings, and excruciating lashes from whips. His fellow Jews hated him, while many Christians still feared him because of the persecution he had organized against the church. He was opposed and rejected by so many.

After opening 2 Corinthians by describing his deep pain and shedding light on some of the conflict in his relationship with the Corinthians, Paul wrote, "Therefore, having this ministry by the mercy of God, we do not lose heart" (4:1). The ministry that God had entrusted to Paul gave him hope. Amid the suffering and conflicts, a sense of ministry purpose enabled him to persevere hopefully.

In the next chapter, he further coalesced his frank longing for deliverance with his hopeful resolution to serve God while he waited for glory:

> So we are always of good courage. We know that while we are at home in the body we are away from the Lord, for we walk by faith, not by sight. Yes, we are of good courage, and we would rather be away from the body and at home with the Lord. So whether we are at home or away, we make it our aim to please him. For we must all appear before the judgment seat of Christ, so that each one may receive what is due for what he has done in the body, whether good or evil. (2 Cor. 5:6–10)

The desire to serve and please the Lord kept Paul hanging on. The thought of going before the judgment seat of God, where he would present a life of service as an offering to Christ, inspired him. Paul wanted to store up treasure in heaven.

Paul concisely summed up this same notion in Philippians 1:21: "*To live is Christ and to die is gain.*" To Paul, dying was preferable; it was a step into experiencing the fullness of union with Christ. He acknowledged that he was "hard pressed" between wanting to remain on earth versus ascending into heaven (Phil. 1:23).

The apostle concluded that staying on earth in order to love and serve Jesus constituted the better, ultimate option. He wrote that remaining in the flesh "means fruitful labor for me" (Phil. 1:22).

In other words, Paul says, "I want to be alive because I want to serve God and others." Many bereaved believers would consider it a miracle to be able to say these words, given the sorrow of their circumstances. Paul's clarity on God's purpose for his life enabled him to endure with hope.

Tragedy Cannot Deter Your God-Given Purpose

When God created mankind, he made us with a purpose. In Genesis 1 and 2, when the writer records the creation of Adam and Eve, we see purpose and meaning inherent in God's design for people. God made people to live in communion with him and with each other. He made them to fill and subdue the earth. God intended for people to cultivate his creation for his glory.

After the fall of man in Genesis 3, when Adam and Eve disobeyed God, the nature of man's purpose changed, but the mission-oriented fabric of humanity did not. Sin fractured man's relationship with God, creation, self, and other people. As a result, God's mission, which we see as the dominant storyline in the Bible, is to reconcile all things in heaven and earth to himself until the world becomes a perfect place.

The Lord did not decide to snap his finger and instantly fix the problem. Instead, for whatever reason, he chose to perform this mission of restoration and redemption through human beings. He first attempted this mission through the Israelites, whom he made to be a "kingdom of priests and a holy nation" (Ex. 19:6). Through their moral purity, kindness to the poor, justice for the oppressed, and worship of their merciful and holy God, the Lord intended to draw all nations to himself. However, the Israelites failed miserably.

The story of the New Testament involves God doing through Christ what Israel failed to accomplish. Paul described the Lord's purpose and will, which he performed through Christ, as "unit[ing] all things in him, things in heaven and things on earth" (Eph. 1:9–10). Jesus's life, death, and resurrection set off the total remediation of all effects of the fall, which will culminate at Christ's second coming, when he makes the world perfect again. Until then, God has sent his Holy Spirit to work through the lives of people for his redemptive mission in the world.

Why am I offering this brief biblical history of redemption?

When the Worst comes, you feel as if the storyline and purpose of your life have either been seriously disrupted or totally terminated. Before the Worst, you had dreams and aspirations. Now tragedy and pain have shattered your vision.

As the tides of sadness flow through your heart, it is natural to feel as if the waves have carried away the purpose of your life. Many people experience a disorienting sense of apathy and purposelessness in the wake of their Worst.

However, we must believe that no tragedy possesses more force and determination than God's plan of redemption for the world. No disappointment can expunge the inherent mission that God envisioned when he conceived your life. No trial can extract you from the redemptive narrative that Christ called you into when he saved your soul and enlisted you in his redemptive mission. No difficulty can nullify the intrinsic purpose inherent in God designing you.

In fact, your Worst further equips you uniquely for this mission. God's mission involves remediating the effects of the fall. This means that Christian mission fundamentally engages sadness, injustice, poverty, depression, despair, sickness, grief, and death. God's mission is a work of healing, and no healing can occur without seeing and touching the wounds.

Your Worst deepens your capacity to enter into and confront the brokenness in the world around you. As the Lord heals your heart, you gain a strength, toughness, and courage that did not previously exist. You inherit greater compassion and empathy for other sufferers because you understand their pain more deeply than you did before your Worst.

In some cases, doctors say that when a bone breaks, it grows back stronger. Indeed, when we allow the Lord to heal our heart after our Worst, our mission in the world grows back with added strength and fortitude.

Furthermore, your wounds become credentials that give you credibility and trustworthiness as you minister to those who share your common suffering. Before my son died, I had very little to offer parents who had lost children. Since Cam passed away, God has opened many doors for me to care for people in the same situation.

We all know how this works. People who have not experienced our same sort of tragedy can help, but their comfort and advice only go so far. We all value the wisdom and compassion of those who have gone before us, those who truly know what we are going through. If you struggle with mental illness, you want to talk to someone with your same condition. If you have cancer, you want to talk to a survivor. If you've had a miscarriage, you want to talk to a woman who has experienced one too.

Again, your wounds become your credentials. They serve as a card that grants you access and entry into the lives and sadness of other people. In time, after you have started to heal and recover, the Lord will expand your mission field. You can become "that person" who shows up for, listens to, advises, and cares for others. When people with the same struggle or tragedy say, "Nobody understands," you have the credibility to respond, "I do."

At the same time, we must exercise caution. This new ministry that comes out of our Worst can become an idol that we use to escape our pain or to justify our loss. This ministry can become a means by which we try to fix ourselves.

At times, I felt as if helping enough people after Cam died would in some way make my tragedy feel worth it. In reality, I started to have a false expectation that serving others out of my tragedy would heal me. Only God's grace in God's time can heal us.

Still, what I want you to know is that your life continues to have meaning and purpose on the other side of your Worst. In fact, that sense of meaning and purpose only deepens if we allow God to heal us and then open ourselves to the redemptive call of God in a broken world.

Service in Your Worst Nightmare

The quandary you are facing in the season of your Worst centers on the question of meaning. *What is the point of life? Why am I miserable here when this all could be over in heaven?* Your questions intensify when your worst nightmare involves the death of a loved one, because you want to be with them, and they presumably are in heaven.

First, you need to understand that having these difficulties and questions is not abnormal. Many people in tragedy struggle to find a reason to take the next step and to live another day. You do not need to feel ashamed by these feelings.

Simultaneously, you do not have to remain defeated: There is a reason for you to live. God ordained a purpose for your life before the foundation of the world. Your Worst did not come as a surprise to him and does not constitute the end of his appointed mission for your life. In fact, your Worst most likely factors into and enhances the redemptive works that God has prepared in advance for you to do (Eph. 2:10). God began a "good work in you" that *he* will complete on the day of Christ Jesus—not on the day of your Worst (Phil. 1:6). Nothing can disrupt God's eternal purposes for your life.

God may give you opportunities to serve people who experience a trauma similar to yours. God undoubtedly will increase your capacity for empathy and compassion for all who suffer. You will be able to love and care for others better. You now have knowledge, experience, and credibility in an area that you probably never wanted, but your trial will make you into a vessel of hope and comfort for someone else down the road.

While you eventually will again find meaning in things such as work and hobbies, the kind of meaning that you need in your Worst is the type that enables you to get out of bed in the morning. This kind of meaning comes most assuredly from things related to the love and service of God and neighbor. Kingdom-related service connects most directly to the intrinsic design with which God made you. It connects to the core of your soul and ignites that God-given reality that your life is valuable and worth living.

It may take months or years before your feet land on the ground after your Worst, but God will give you meaning and joy in the new horizons of love and service that he has in store. God will supply you with a reason to get out of bed in the morning.

The Narrative of Hope

My life is not over. God has purposes and plans for me in this life until I enter into his paradise. He will use me to love and serve people. He may use my Worst as an avenue to comfort others who might share in a similar suffering in the future. God has purpose and meaning in every day of my life until he calls me home. I will live by faith and entrust my life to his service. He will give me joy and hope as I serve him and bear fruit for his kingdom.

He will wipe away every tear from their eyes, and death shall be no more, neither shall there be mourning, nor crying, nor pain anymore, for the former things have passed away.

Revelation 21:4

12

Heaven

In Greek mythology, no character embodies the nature of eternal misery like that of Sisyphus. While many versions of the story exist, their consistent theme is that Sisyphus was an unscrupulous and avaricious king who repeatedly used deceit for self-glory. King Sisyphus exercised particularly poor judgment when he tried to use his cleverness to outsmart the gods.

After Sisyphus betrayed a secret of Zeus (king of the Greek gods), Zeus deployed Thanatos (death personified) to banish Sisyphus to Tartarus, a deep place of torment in the underworld. However, the sly Sisyphus used his guile to turn the tables on Thanatos, whom Sisyphus chained up in Tartarus. As a result, no one on earth could die, causing a painful problem, especially for the old and suffering.

For this treachery, Zeus sentenced Sisyphus to an eternity of pushing a large boulder up a hill, only to have the massive stone roll back down just as he nearly reached the top. In the myth, Sisyphus repeats this futile labor for eternity.

The story of Sisyphus captures the Greek ideal of ultimate torment. One strives and pushes to the point of near relief, only to be sent back to the base of the hill to restart the agonizing process again. Forever.

When the Worst comes upon you, it feels as if your life has been transformed into a marathon without a finish line. Many marathon runners will say that the euphoria of crossing the finish line and feeling the sense of gratification and relief outweighs the grueling discomfort of the 26.2 miles of hard running, not to mention the months of training. However, if you take the finish line away, then the marathon becomes torture. It becomes nothing but pain and despair.

God knows that strugglers in the fallen world need a finish line. In Genesis 3, after Adam and Eve ate from the tree and committed that fatal sin, he banished them from the garden. Often people exclusively view this motion as God's judgment against the first couple. However, a closer look reveals the mercy in this act. God knew that if they ate from the tree of life, they would never die. They would remain on earth—struggling and suffering and longing—until Christ returned and restored the world. They would face thousands of years without any hope of short-term relief. Hence, God protected Adam and Eve by going to measured lengths to prevent them from reentering the garden and eating from the tree of life. God created a finish line by ensuring that they ultimately would die and leave the fallen world.

Heaven plays a critical role in the mind-set of a person living in their Worst. It does not just function as a finish line; it also serves as the certain comfort and reassurance for your heart.

The Fulfillment of Every Heart's Desire

In John 14–18, Jesus prepared the disciples for the hardships and challenges ahead. He knew that they would witness his hostile arrest and violent crucifixion. He knew that the disciples would see the darkness in themselves as they turned their backs on him. He knew that they would have to cope with life without his physical presence. He also knew that most, as they embarked on their apostolic ministries, would face persecution and resistance to the point of death. On a positive note, they would see Christ resurrected and they would receive the Holy Spirit, but the trauma and severity of their trials would surpass what most people ever encounter. In these passages, John shares the lessons Jesus offers his beloved friends to prepare them for the difficult road ahead.

In John 14, Jesus focused on a central spoke in their axis of hope: heaven. Christ told the disciples to not let their "hearts be troubled" (John 14:1). He explained that "in [his] Father's house are many rooms" and that he goes before them "to prepare a place for [them]" (John 14:2). Christ promised a perfect future home in order to sustain them in their forthcoming trials.

What makes this new home such a vibrant source of hope? First, Christ told the disciples that he would come for them and take them to be with him. He sang of the greatest longing of the heart: to experience perfect, everlasting fellowship with God.

So often we think in our Worst that if our circumstances were different, then we would be content. *If this tragedy or difficulty were not in my life, then I would be satisfied.* In reality, whether you face tragedy or not, nothing will be enough until that day when you see Christ face-to-face and live as one with him for eternity. You were made for paradise and will not be satisfied until you experience it. Jesus guarantees that this euphoric day awaits us.

Jesus's promise to the disciples also means that Christ will rescue them from the misery of the fallen world. All our pain and suffering flow from the rebellion of Eden. As long as we dwell on earth, we never will outrun the fallout from Adam and Eve's divine violation. But Jesus will deliver us! He will take us away! In heaven, we will be eternally insulated from every bad thing that came as a result of the fall: sickness, depression, sadness, violence, warfare, starvation, divorce, abuse, death—all of it. When Jesus takes us to that heavenly place, our exposure to brokenness and pain will end permanently.

A part of our release from the external or environmental aspect of the fall includes a permanent divorce from our own sin and flesh. When we enter Christ's heavenly kingdom, God will glorify us and prevent us from ever being able to sin again. The internal temptations of lust, greed, anger, resentment, hatred, and envy will become foreign experiences for eternity. We never again will fight battles with addiction, doubt, compulsion, bitterness, and anxiety. We will escape self-manufactured pain forever.

Set Your Mind on Your Home

For the marathon runner, the finish line represents everything. It is relief from the painful discomfort of the grueling race. It is the ecstasy of accomplishment. It is the celebration and hugs and story-sharing with the other finishers.

Heaven is our finish line, and the apostle Paul tells us to set our minds and hearts on the ticker tape in the distance. Paul reminds us to "seek the things that are above, where Christ is, seated at the right hand of God" (Col. 3:1). He further exhorts us to "set [our] minds on things that are above, not on things that are on earth" (Col. 3:2). The nature of the imperative verbs that Paul uses in these instructions is not that of a one-time command. He calls for us to continually point our hearts and minds to heaven, such that eternity becomes an active part of our daily consciousness.

The more we set our mind on "things above," the more patience and endurance we receive during our Worst. Meditating on heaven establishes a true context for our tribulation. Eternity becomes a more real, tangible backdrop for the trials of our lives.

Setting our minds on eternity reminds us that we are not meant for this fallen world. We were made to live in the garden of Eden in unbroken fellowship with God, humanity, and the cosmos. When heaven maintains a central place in our consciousness, it reminds us that we were made for more than this earth. John Calvin commented that God uses our sufferings to remind us of this fact. He wrote:

> Whatever kind of tribulation with which we are afflicted, we should always consider the end of it to be, that we may be trained to despise the present, and thereby stimulated to aspire to the future life.[11]

When we forget our heavenly home, we tend to think that this life is all there is; life on earth constitutes all of existence. When you are facing tragedy, can there be a worse thought? Can you imagine being stuck in this miserable place forever? But this is a temporary life, described as a vapor by the writer of Ecclesiastes; we were made for so much more. This is a phase—like middle school (perish the thought)—and God offers something far greater and far, far, far more permanent in our future.

The apostles practiced an eternal mind-set. What one sees in Scripture is that the apostolic writers saw life as very, very short. Peter, when writing to Christians undergoing religious persecution in Asia Minor, said that our suffering on earth would last for a "little while" (1 Pet. 5:10). In 2 Corinthians, Paul said that he suffered to such a degree that he thought he had "received the sentence of death" and "despaired of life itself" (2 Cor. 1:8–9). At the beginning of this same letter, he was in so much pain that he thought he would die. And yet, at the same time, in chapters 4 and 5 where Paul talks about the hope and glory of heaven, he now refers to these same trials as "light momentary affliction" (2 Cor. 4:17). When Paul views his Worst through the context of eternity, it is effectively the snap of a finger.

The question I repeatedly asked after Cam died was, "How am I going to make it through life without him?" Each of the first days of grief felt like a week, and each month felt like a year. In those early days, my perceived miserable future seemed everlasting.

You may feel the same way in the early days of your Worst and beyond. Regardless of the nature of your trial, you cannot imagine walking another ten, twenty, thirty, forty, or fifty years with these shards of the shattered glass in your feet that make you wince with every step. You must remember, first, that God redeems. In time, as you trust him, the Lord will heal your heart. At the same time, the remnant of your Worst always will reside to some degree. I never completely will outrun Cam's absence in this life. Still, the more we "set [our] minds on things above," the shorter the trial seems (Col. 3:2). When we compare this life to the trillions of years of utter ecstasy we will experience with Christ and with a fully healed heart, we see that our trials comparatively will last as long as a burning matchstick.

Nothing Will Be Lost

Any person who has lost a child will tell you about the most complicated, painful, stressful question you can get asked after your child's death. The question comes from a stranger with no ill intent. It happens at the swings at the park or at story time or at the pediatrician's office. Perhaps it comes at a grocery store or a coffee shop or a party or on an airplane.

You're doing fine, and then a person utters *that* question. You start to feel nervous, as if you now are on a stage about to deliver a speech. Butterflies swarm inside. That wound in your heart gets strained, as if you stepped wrong again on a sprained ankle. The analytical part of your brain kicks into high gear, thinking, *How will I answer this time?* while you consider multiple angles.

"How many children do you have?"

That's the question.

If I say three, referring to my three children on earth, am I betraying my child in heaven? If I say three, am I opening up the door for an awkward and painful conversation with a stranger?

I decided early on, for the sake of my hope, that I would always include Cam in the number. It reminds me that my son lives. He's not with me, but he's alive and never has been better. Cam has a vibrant life. He plays and dances and sings. He has friends and a perfect Father who snuggles with him and tells him stories and rejoices over him to a degree of which I am totally incapable.

It also reminds me that I have a future with Cam in the life that he currently enjoys in heaven. So much of my grief involves the loss of experiences. There are the first football games, the birthday parties, the graduations, and father-son trips that I never will enjoy with him in *this life*. Remembering that he is still my son and that he is still alive reminds me that nothing truly will be lost, and everything I've lost in this life will be recovered in the life to come.

I will see my little boy again. We will have a beautiful, fun, intimate, joyful life together for eternity in heaven. We will have adventures and lessons and laughter and meals and celebrations. We will hug and snuggle and kiss and laugh and play in heaven. Perhaps we will even be able to play rounds of golf and go on hikes and throw a baseball and swim in rivers in the new earth.

For people suffering the death of a loved one, a common lament is the loss of all the experiences with that person. Every holiday or special occasion or milestone becomes a monument of his or her absence and what you missed out on together.

But God offers us sufferers a promise of experiences for eternity. For the mother who miscarried a baby girl, you will brush and braid her hair one day. To the father of the stillborn son, you will wrestle with your little man in the future. To the parents of a child with cerebral palsy, you will run and jump and dance with your healed child on the streets of the New Jerusalem. To the widow whose husband died as you were just beginning that long-awaited season of retirement, the vacations and quality time that you missed do await you in heaven.

For some in the midst of their worst nightmare, the prospect of heaven troubles them. They have lost a loved one and question whether that person will be in heaven because they never outwardly professed faith in Christ. If this is your situation, I offer you two words of comfort. First, you are not God. You do not know the full extent of the prayers that person may have prayed in his or her heart or what happened in the last moments of life. Second, in heaven you will be satisfied with the outcome. Hard to believe, but you *will* be at peace.

If you are a person who is uncertain about heaven as your final resting place, please don't leave this great hope in doubt any longer. If you assume that you've lived a good life and that will cover it, don't be deceived. You don't have *real*, certain hope. The way to certainty about heaven is through reconciliation with God.

It starts by simply coming to God and having a conciliatory conversation. You tell God you're sorry for the things you've done wrong. Tell him that you want to be forgiven and that you want to be in a relationship with him now and forever. And then thank God for sending Jesus to make this reconciliation possible. Reconciliation with God through Christ closes the door on any lack of clarity about whether or not God will accept you. As the apostle John said, "If we confess our sins, he is faithful and just to forgive us our sins and to cleanse us from all unrighteousness" (1 John 1:9). Reconciliation with God enables you to make heaven the expected, certain hope of your heart.

The Second Coming

I long to be in heaven. I long to be delivered from all pain and suffering. I long to be permanently filled with joy. I long to be with my son again. I long to see Jesus face-to-face. But I long for even more, and so does Christ.

When Christians think about heaven, they ordinarily focus on what we call the "intermediate state." This is the perfect place where believers in Christ go immediately upon death. "Heaven" is not the end, though. The marriage of heaven and earth, initiated by Christ's second coming, constitutes God's highest aim. Christ ultimately will return to earth and bring heaven with him. He will rid the earth of all pain, sorrow, and brokenness. He will banish all wickedness, injustice, and evil.

In Revelation, martyrs in heaven who were killed for their faith repeatedly ask Jesus, "O Sovereign Lord, holy and true, how long before you will judge and avenge our blood on those who dwell on the earth?" (6:9). These people are in heaven, and yet they still long for the earth's restoration. They want all crooked things to be made right.

If your suffering has come as a product of abuse, violence, persecution, or exploitation, as the martyrs in heaven, you struggle with the question of justice and retribution. You want to see the wicked things in the world fully rectified. You long for a day when God straightens out all this crookedness.

The church at Thessalonica faced intense persecution and resistance in its first generation. The apostle Paul knew the fear, anger, and despair that these young Christians experienced in the face of religious oppression. He offered them this comfort:

> Indeed God considers it just to repay with affliction those who afflict you, and to grant relief to you who are afflicted as well as to us, when the Lord Jesus is revealed from heaven with his mighty angels. (2 Thess. 1:6–7)

The central desire to which Paul speaks and for which every heart yearns is the complete remediation of all the effects of sin. Whether those effects involve cancer, trisomy 18, heart attacks, miscarriages, car accidents, tornadoes, hurricanes, violence, human trafficking, abuse, addictions—anything that is plainly wrong and at odds with Eden—God will renounce and eliminate forever.

Horatio Spafford was an American businessman who lost four children at once when a ship carrying his family sank in the Atlantic Ocean in 1873. On his journey across the ocean waters to see where his daughters died, Spafford wrote the classic hymn "It Is Well with My Soul." In this song, Spafford relates the truths of Christ that enabled him to have peace in the midst of horrific tragedy. He finishes the hymn with this stanza:

> And Lord, haste the day when my faith shall be sight,
> The clouds be rolled back as a scroll;
> The trump shall resound, and the Lord shall descend,
> A song in the night, oh my soul!

My soul too yearns for Christ's return. It is not enough for me—and not enough for God—that I personally will receive relief in heaven while people continue to suffer on earth. I long for the time when Jesus completely eradicates from this world all death, mourning, pain, and suffering. God promises this day in Revelation 21:1–4, the second-to-last chapter of the Bible:

> Then I saw a new heaven and a new earth, for the first heaven and the first earth had passed away, and the sea was no more. And I saw the holy city, new Jerusalem, coming down out of heaven from God, prepared as a bride adorned for her husband. And I heard a loud voice from the throne saying, "Behold, the dwelling place of God is with man. He will dwell with them, and they will be his people, and God himself will be with them as their God. He will wipe away every tear from their eyes, and death shall be no more, neither shall there be mourning, nor crying, nor pain anymore, for the former things have passed away."

And on that day, I will run to the children's hospital with a sledgehammer and tear down every wall, because we will no longer need a place for sick children nor a place where they may die. Christ will have vanquished sickness and death.

Then I will sprint with Cam to his former grave at Elmwood Cemetery, and I will dance and spit on and taunt the empty hole where my son used to be buried. I will mock death in the name of Jesus. That cemetery will become a place of beauty because Christ has fully redeemed creation; and, on that day, death will be no more.

Heaven in Your Worst Nightmare

In this long journey of suffering, there is hope that a day will come when God completely eliminates your misery. It will all be over. No tears, no anxiety, no bitterness. You will be fully healed. Heaven is a real place that God has prepared for you. You will escape the fall and experience perfect union with God forever.

Because heaven constitutes the bedrock of your hope, meditate on it often. Imagine the rich life God has in store for you with him in eternity. It will remind you that your Worst is temporary and short relative to the blessed eternity awaiting you. It will remind you that you were made for another place and created for so much more. It will remind you that God will bring forth a day when everything that is crooked will be made straight, and everything hurt will be healed.

The Narrative of Hope

My ultimate home is in heaven. There I will live in perfect bliss and peace forever. God will eliminate all my pain and misery. Many reunions await me in heaven with friends and family. In heaven, I will see Jesus face-to-face and he will hold me forever in perfect comfort. With every day I live, I move one step closer to my ultimate home of absolute joy and peace. God ultimately will bring heaven to earth and will eliminate sin, sorrow, and brokenness forever.

The Narrative of Hope

The road ahead of me is long and painful, but Christ has defeated sin and death through the cross. I can face reality and make this journey, because on the other side of the cross is the resurrection. In the same way that Christ rose from the dead, so too can my life emerge from the darkness into light. The gospel tells me that I cannot redeem myself; only Christ can heal and free my heart. My only hope is to trust him to do so. My tragedy has not disrupted the narrative of my life. My story remains God's story, and that is a story of redemption. (*Gospel*)

Christ claimed that he was God. He claimed that he could forgive sins. He claimed that he will redeem the world. He rose from the dead and proved his promises to be true. God's promises of redemption are not wishful fantasies. They are real, relevant, and powerful promises based on an event in history. If God has the ability to raise Jesus from the dead, then he can redeem all of my suffering and misery. The life of my Worst is buried with Christ in death and will be raised with him in resurrection power. (*Resurrection*)

My need is so deep; I am desperate for help. God longs to be gracious to me. He rises up to show me compassion. He has called me to focus only on this hour, only on this day. The Lord deeply loves me. He is on my side. Out of this loves comes his burning desire to help me. I can call on him, and he will give me just the grace I need for this hour of darkness. He will supply the grace for the next step. The life, death, and resurrection of Jesus assure me that God cares for me and that he will go to the greatest extent to meet my need. (*Grace*)

Even though I dwell in darkness and anguish, God can rescue me. I am not called to redeem myself. I am called to shift my burden to Jesus and to trust him to deliver me from this pain and despair. God can do it, and I can rely on him to be my redeemer. (*Faith*)

God understands my suffering. He lived as a vulnerable, afflicted human being in Jesus Christ. When I cry, he cries. When my heart breaks, his heart breaks. I can trust him as a fellow sufferer who empathizes with me. (*Empathy*)

I am not alone. I may feel isolated, but the Lord never will turn his back on me. Nothing I can do will make him walk away. In my suffering, Jesus draws near to me. God always remains at my side, and I remain in his arms forever. Nothing can stand between the Lord and me. (*Presence*)

Bitterness is my biggest enemy in the season of my worst nightmare. I am a sinner to whom God owes nothing. I am not entitled to anything and cannot resent God. God is not punishing me. Jesus removed whatever judgment I earned through my sins. In spite of my sin, God loves me through Christ. (*Sin*)

My trial is not a random accident. Nothing comes into my life but through God's perfect discretion. God remains in control of all circumstances. He has a hand in my painful circumstances, which means that his hand can extend to redeem my life. God is good. The evil in this world and the suffering in my circumstances do not represent his character. The perfectly kind and loving person, Jesus Christ, is the very image of the character of God. I can trust him, knowing that he is fully good and fully in control. (*Providence*)

When I am confused and frustrated, I can express these feelings to God. I can share my doubts with him. I am a human being and not capable of fully comprehending why my child died. God knows this; he loves and accepts me anyway. I can be honest with God. Never will I have a satisfactory explanation in this life, but I take comfort knowing that God is good and his ways are perfect. (*Doubt*)

My life is not over; my despair not permanent. I can have joy today—in this moment—through the presence of Christ. God can turn all my sorrow into joy, all my mourning into gladness, all my crying into dancing. Christ is making all things new. In his time, he can redeem the entirety of my pain and grief and give me a joyful life. (*Joy*)

My life is not over. God has purposes and plans for me in this life until I enter into his paradise. He will use me to love and serve people. He may use my Worst as an avenue to comfort others who might share in a similar suffering in the future. God has purpose and meaning in every day of my life until he calls me home. I will live by faith and entrust my life to his service. He will give me joy and hope as I serve him and bear fruit for his kingdom. (*Service*)

My ultimate home is in heaven. There I will live in perfect bliss and peace forever. God will eliminate all my pain and misery. Many reunions await me in heaven with friends and family. In heaven, I will see Jesus face-to-face and he will hold me forever in perfect comfort. With every day I live, I move one step closer to my ultimate home of absolute joy and peace. God ultimately will bring heaven to earth and forever eliminate sin, sorrow, and brokenness. (*Heaven*)

Epilogue

Three months after Cam died, we learned that we were unexpectedly pregnant. Getting pregnant during a time of such dark misery was the last thing we intended to do. As the first trimester concluded, we discovered that this new baby was a boy.

In mid-November at 1:30 a.m., Lauren nudged me and announced that her water had broken. We raced to the hospital. There was no time for an epidural. Our third child and second son, William Hutchins Cole IV, was born fifty-two minutes after Lauren's water broke, seventeen minutes after her admission to the hospital.

On November 13, 2013, we had buried our precious son, Cam. On November 13, 2014, the one-year anniversary of Cam's funeral, God brought new life into our family.

God is real. God is good. Christ reigns forever.

Acknowledgments

The writing of this book has been the joy of a lifetime amid immense darkness. There are an endless number of people who have contributed to making this book possible and to whom I owe thanks and recognition.

First, I could never have done this without my host of "friendship editors." Charlotte Botsford, for getting this project off the ground and being a true sister; you are amazing at writing and friendship. To Mary Berkeley Pritchard and Emily Price for being faithful, precise proofreaders. To "Coach" Kathy Lawrence, what an incredible season it was working through the final draft; I'll never forget our meetings or the brilliant help you provided. To Collin Hansen and Nancy Guthrie for honest, invaluable feedback and direction.

Second, thanks must be given to the amazing Cathedral Church of the Advent. To the whole church, for supporting my family and me through this entire season. To the youth group, for being so courageous and compassionate and such a ray of hope for me. To Dean Pearson, for giving me time and permission to write this. To Victor, Mary, John, Virginia, and the choir for the beautiful musical tributes to Cam.

Next, thanks to our amazing friends who carried us through a gut-wrenching season of grief and a long season of writing. To our small group, you simply are the best. To the Cam's Corner Team, I'll never forget what you did for us. To my prayer team, for your many petitions. To the Heavy Hitters, for always making me smile. To the unsurpassed Dr. Stacey Gilbert and Dr. Joe Larussa, for being so helpful and steady always and in every way. To the Rooted team, for your support and presence. To the youth staff, thank you for your friendship and for the immense load you have carried for me. To all of our friends who have wept with us and never forgotten Cam, we thank you.

I must express deep gratitutde to my wife, Lauren, for allowing me to tell our story and for enduring the countless hours I invested in this project. I also need to thank Mary Matthews and Hutch for being my proud cheerleaders and source of inspiration!

Finally, this project would be dead in the water without Dave DeWit of Crossway. Thank you, Dave, for believing in this book and advocating for it from the very beginning. I'll forever be indebted to you for making this project happen.

Notes

1. People have debated whether grace means God's attitude of unearned favor toward mankind or if it constitutes the actual help that God gives. A comprehensive reading of the Bible suggests that grace encompasses both God's favorable disposition toward his people *and* the actual help that God extends to us. It's a "both–and" concept.
2. Robert Wuthnow, *After the Baby Boomers: How Twenty- and Thirty-Somethings Are Shaping the Future of American Religion* (Princeton, NJ: Princeton University Press, 2010), 14.
3. Anthony Thiselton, *First Epistle to the Corinthians: The New International Greek Testament Commentary* (Grand Rapids, MI: Eerdmans, 2000).
4. "'We Are Not the Same People,' Say Rick and Kay Warren about Losing Their Son," Assist News Service Online, March 25, 2015, http://kaywarren.com/article/we-are-not-the-same-people-say-rick-and-kay-warren-about-losing-their-son/.
5. "Carry On" featuring Fun, track 4 on *Some Nights*, TommyD & Jeff Bhasker, October 23, 2012, compact disc.
6. Kenneth Laing Harris and August Konkel, "Job," The ESV Study Bible®, ESV® Bible (Wheaton, IL: Crossway, 2008), 910.
7. The Archbishop of Canterbury preached this sermon at Child Bereavement UK's Christmas Carol Service at HTB Church in London on December 10, 2015.

8. Tim Keller, "The Doctrine of Salvation" (sermon, July 4, 2004), https://gospelinlife.com/downloads/the-doctrine-of-salvation-5365.
9. "40" featuring U2, track 10 in *War*, Steve Lillywhite, Windmill Lane Studios, Dublin, 1983.
10. John Claypool, *Tracks of a Fellow Struggler: Living and Growing through Grief* (New York: Moorehouse, 1995), 80.
11. John Calvin, *The Institutes of the Christian Religion* (Grand Rapids, MI: Eerdmans, 1995), 25.

General Index

Scripture Index